Under the Open Sky

The Paintings of the Newlyn and Lamorna Artists 1880–1940 in the Public Collections of Cornwall and Plymouth

Catherine Wallace

Truran

First published in 2002 by Truran, Croft Prince, Mount Hawke, Truro, Cornwall TR4 8EE
www.truranbooks.co.uk

ISBN 1 85022 168 5

Printed and bound in Cornwall by R Booth Ltd,
Antron Hill, Mabe, Penryn, Cornwall TR10 9HH

Author's Acknowledgments
I would like to thank Dr Melissa Hardie for all her assistance in accessing the West Cornwall Art Archive and the Newyln Art Gallery archive. To Alan Shears of Shears Fine Art for allowing me access to his wonderful collection of photographs. I must also thank all the curators of the four museums in Cornwall and Plymouth for allowing me to view their collections even when not on public display. In particular I would like to thank Katie Herbert from Penlee House for her patience and assistance. Thanks to George Bednar for his eye to detail and all the authors and researchers of the many books and exhibition catalogues on Newlyn and Lamorna artists, which have been the bedrock of this book. Thanks go to my partner Jonathan Craig for his patience and support in reading and editing the book and to the publishers Heather and Ivan Corbett for their positive attitude.

Publisher's Acknowledgments
The publishers thank the curators and staff of the four galleries in Cornwall and Plymouth. Particular thanks are due to Alison Lloyd and Katie Herbert of Penlee House Gallery and Museum, Penzance for their support, help and advice.

Contents

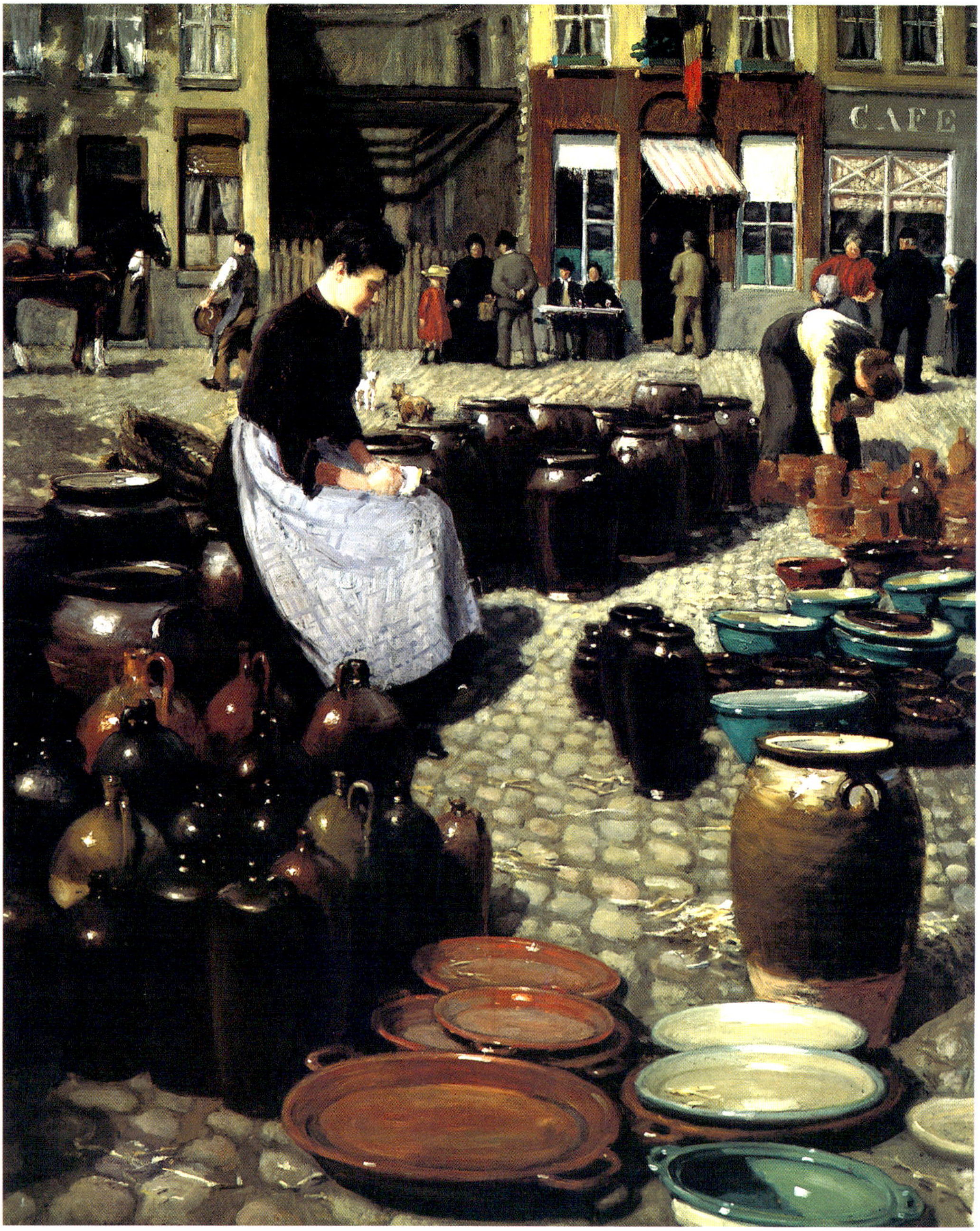

1
Norman Garstin
Among the Pots
date unknown
oil on canvas
127.5x102.5cm
(Plymouth City Museum and Art Gallery)

Introduction: An Artistic Melting Pot

'The Newlyners are the most significant body of painters now in England' [1]

The Newlyners were a group of artists who gained their name from making a small fishing village at the south-western tip of Cornwall their home and their inspiration. They had a common approach to painting. They worked mainly outdoors in front of the subject whether it be landscape, seascape or figures. The French painter Jules Bastien-Lepage (1848–1884) was the major influence for this approach. Although only 36 when he died in 1884, Bastien-Lepage had achieved both fame and respect for his paintings of figures in landscapes mostly created outdoors, known as *plein air* painting. The other feature, which distinguished the Newlyners from many British artists at the time, was their particular method of painting known as the 'square brush technique'. This allowed the artist to be less distracted by detail when applying the paint and to move across the canvas more quickly, thus adding vitality to the making of marks on the canvas.

These continental ideas came as a result of the Newlyners' studies in the studios or ateliers of Paris, Antwerp and Munich. Those who went to France had a particularly wide experience, working with artists from New Zealand, Scandinavia, America and Australia. Not all the Newlyners painted outdoors, neither did they all practise the square brush technique but these are the accepted distinguishing hallmarks of the colony as a whole. Their common theme was in their subject matter: local people and places, fishermen and farm workers, sailors and postmen, all going about their daily lives, and the women: wives and mothers, widows and orphans, young maids and old fishwives. These ordinary people were often used to reflect the hardship of rural life.

Many of the Newlyn artists' colony were friends who had met at English or foreign art schools. They shared a commitment to the same artistic ideas and enjoyed one another's company. There was music and dancing, amateur theatricals and fancy dress parties. Artists lived close to each other or shared accommodation and there was free and easy access to each other's houses and studios.

The backgrounds and experience of the Newlyn artists was very variable – they had mostly had some kind of art education, both in England and on the continent; some settled in Newlyn for long periods while others came and went.

In the early 1880s artists such as Walter Langley (1852–1922) and Edwin Harris (1855–1906) left the industrial heartland of England to seek out a more romantic rural location to paint. They were Victorian artists who did not want to paint the nude or the classical stories from ancient Greece or the Bible. They wanted to paint workers' lives. Langley in particular wished to portray the harshness of life for working men and women, even in a picturesque location such as Newlyn. Langley is seen as the pioneer of the Newlyn colony but he never gained the recognition he deserved, largely because his main medium was watercolour, which was not taken as seriously as oil painting by the critics of the time — an attitude that persists.

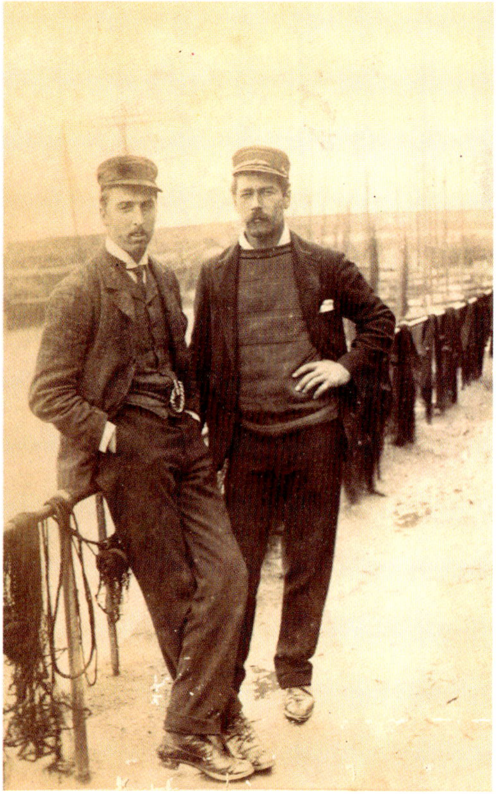

Frank Bramley (1857–1915) studied at Lincoln School of Art and Antwerp and was one of the most important early Newlyn artists. He was a great exponent of the square brush technique which was the hallmark of the first two decades of the colony. His major oil A *Hopeless Dawn* (1888) (Tate Gallery) when shown at the Royal Academy was seen as the most significant Newlyn interior at the time. But it was the arrival of the accomplished Irish painter, Stanhope Alexander Forbes (1857–1947) in 1884 which galvanisd the group of artists into a colony. Forbes painted on the streets, depicting the fishwives and their children and the fishermen mending their nets and selling fish on the beach, as well as festivals and holidays. His painting *Fish Sale on a Cornish Beach* (1884) (Plymouth) was praised by the critics at the Royal Academy and put the Newlyn colony of artists on the art world stage. With the equally talented Canadian artist Elizabeth Armstrong (1859–1912) whom he had married in 1889, Stanhope Forbes was the focus of the group. Elizabeth Armstrong had studied art in London, America and Munich and produced some fine etchings and watercolours establishing her as an artist in her own right before she married.

2
Photo of Tuke & Chevallier Tayler (Penlee House Gallery and Museum, on loan from The Cornwall Centre)

3
Some of the Newlyn artists on the sea front (Penlee House Gallery and Museum, on loan from The Cornwall Centre)

Stanhope Forbes taught his philosophy of *plein air* painting for 50 years from 1889–1939 at the Forbes' school of painting which he ran firstly with Elizabeth and then after her death with his second wife, Maudie. He is recognised as the father of the Newlyn colony. His own work reflected some of the changes in the international art scene moving from Realism to a moderate form of Impressionism, but he was never in favour of modern art. Thus the Forbes' painting school set the tone for the second generation of Newlyn artists. Through the school, Stanhope Forbes had a great influence on many of the artists who studied under him. He attracted other artists to come to paint in and around Newlyn. One such artist was Samuel John 'Lamorna' Birch (1869–1955), who when visiting the area fell in love with Lamorna Valley along the coast from Newlyn. He became the main influence and leading artist in a second generation of visiting artists who came to Cornwall between 1910 and 1940 including Laura (1877–1970) and Harold Knight (1874–1961) and Alfred Munnings (1878–1959). Many of the artists who came to study at the Forbes' school met and married choosing to stay on to live and work near Lamorna including Ernest (1886–1935) and Dod Procter (1892–1972), Eleanor (1882–1959) and Robert Hughes (1873–1953), Jill (1890–1966) and Geoffrey Garnier (1889–1970), and the jeweller Ella Champion (1886–1972) who married the painter Charles Naper (1882–1968).

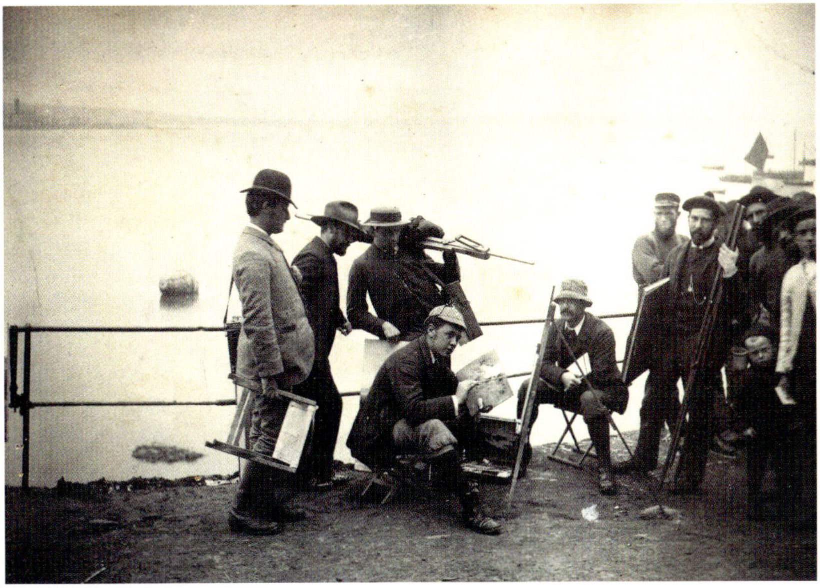

Stanhope Forbes' other significant contribution to the development of Newlyn as an art colony was his role in establishing the Newlyn Art Gallery in 1895. This provided a local exhibition space for the artists, which was often used as a preview prior to their work being exhibited at the Royal Academy. The large paintings of Cornwall and its people were bought for public collections around Britain, Canada, South Africa and Australia. Because of their enlightened buying policy we can see works from Cornwall in some of the major collections of the world, giving the Newlyn and Lamorna art colonies their rightful place in international art history.

This book is an introduction to the art of the Newlyn and Lamorna artists and focuses on the artists' work in the collections of Cornwall and Plymouth.

An important legacy of paintings came from the Newlyn Society of Artists which during the 1970s collected works donated by artists, supporters, collectors and through bequests — since 1991 these have been housed at Penlee House Gallery and Museum in Penzance; Newlyn Art Gallery continues to be an exhibition space for the work of contemporary artists, as was originally intended. Penlee House was made the home of Penzance Town's painting collection in the 1980s and has since then done a great deal to add to its collections. It now boasts one of the largest collections of Newlyn and Lamorna artists in the South-west. It has done much to raise the profile of many of the Cornish painters with major exhibitions in recent years of Walter Langley, Elizabeth Forbes and Harold Harvey.

The important collection at the Royal Cornwall Museum, Truro has been built up over the last 50 years; similarly there have been noteworthy exhibitions on artists and craftspeople of the Newlyn and Lamorna colonies in particular the Cryséde textiles exhibition in 1993 and recently the Thomas Cooper Gotch exhibition in 2001.

Cornwall was not as fortunate as the industrial north of England in having many affluent patrons. However, it was blessed by one particular art benefactor Alfred De Pass

(1861–1952), a South African businessman, who built a holiday residence in Falmouth and gave several large bequests of art and artefacts to Falmouth, Truro and Plymouth Museums.

Falmouth Art Gallery was created in 1978 to house its core collection of paintings given by Alfred De Pass in 1923 and 1939. It has several first class works by Newlyn and Lamorna artists including Henry Scott Tuke (1858–1929), Charles Napier Hemy (1841–1917), Alfred Munnings and Laura Knight. It too has helped to put certain artists back on the art historical map with major exhibitions of the work of Henry Scott Tuke, Charles Napier Hemy and Lamorna Birch. It also raised awareness of the considerable number of highly accomplished women artists in Cornwall who were part of these art colonies.

Just on Cornwall's border lies another major collection of Cornish art at Plymouth City Museum and Art Gallery. It has built up its considerable Newlyn collection over the years with excellent examples of work by Stanhope Forbes, Elizabeth Forbes, Harold Harvey (1874–1941), Norman Garstin (1847–1926), Dod Procter, John Noble Barlow (1861–1917) and Lamorna Birch.

The illustrations in this book are taken from from paintings housed in these South-western galleries; the one is exception is *A Hopeless Dawn* by Frank Bramley (Tate Gallery). Visitors and locals alike can see Newlyn works in the area where they were painted, however the lively exhibition programmes at all four galleries mean that not all the works illustrated are always on display. If a visitor wishes to see a particular painting, it is advisable to telephone the gallery in advance.

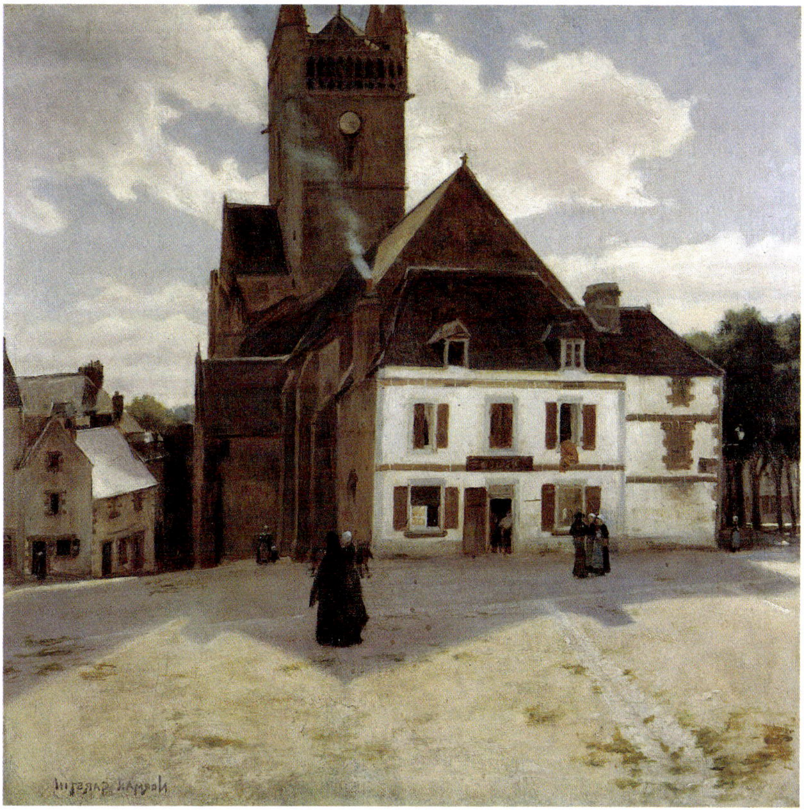

4
Norman Garstin
Church of St Michèle, Quimperlé
c1882
oil on canvas
89.6x89.6cm
(Plymouth City Museum and Art Gallery)

1 Rebellion and Going Continental

The Newlyn artists were seen as rebels – what exactly were they rebelling against?

Victorian art was dominated by work shown at the Royal Academy, the main exhibiting institution. Much was based on classical themes and Bible stories. Artists who depicted the nude, such as Lord Leighton (1830–1896) and Edward Poynter (1836–1919), followed the Greek idealized portrayal of beauty. Theirs was the world of fantasy not reality.

Alongside these classical artists were a group known as the Pre-Raphaelites formed in 1848, whose subjects were based on Arthurian legends and Romantic poetry. The Pre-Raphaelites included William Holman Hunt (1827–1910) and Dante Gabriel Rossetti (1828–82). They were great observers of nature and produced many watercolour studies and sketches on their travels. In the studio these were copied onto canvases in oil in fastidious detail. Their images often included figures in mediaeval costumes from legends or poems.

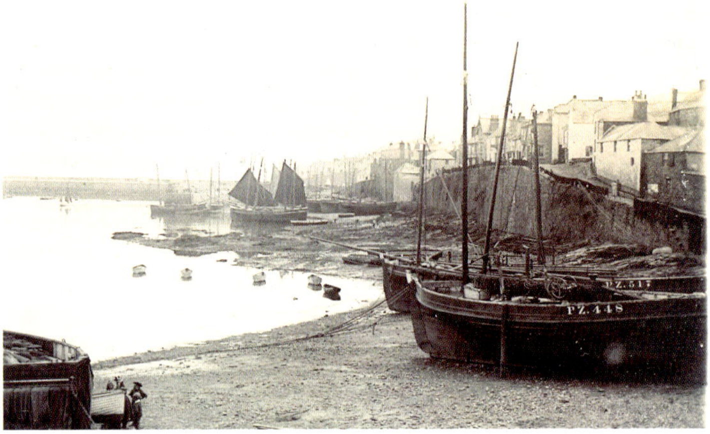

A third strand of art that was developing in Britain at this time turned its back on mythical subjects to depict realistic scenes of Victorian life. Britain and most of northern Europe were at the height of their industrial power. Cities were becoming over-populated as more people left the countryside to work in the factories; there was great poverty and rough living conditions for many. In art, this was reflected in a genre known as Social Realism, where the honest worker was depicted in a romanticized way. Artists such as Ford Madox Brown (1821–1893) and William Powell Frith (1819–1909) painted ordinary people, either the working class or the emerging middle class. Social Realism was a reaction to the subject of the nude usually in a classical or mythological setting, which had been the dominant theme of Victorian painting. In both types of painting there was a strong moral overtone to the work.

Many of the artists who came to Newlyn to paint in the 1880s were reacting to both the Neo-classical and Pre-Raphaelite movements. They were interested in painting ordinary people going about their daily lives. However, their work was inevitably influenced by aspects of British art at the time, as they were all educated in London art schools, where their teachers had a background of Classicism and Aestheticism as well as Social Realism.

Studying art in any form was in its infancy in the 1860s. At that time the Royal Academy was the only institution to offer any formal training. The tutors in the 1870s were artists such as Sir Frederick Leighton, who was President of the Academy from 1878–1896 and Sir Lawrence Alma-Tadema (1836–1912). Both these artists had become renowned for their depictions of classical figures and biblical themes, painted with extraordinary detail. Drawing was taught as a discipline from plaster casts of ancient Greek and Roman sculpture. When the Royal Academy moved to Burlington House in Piccadilly, a design school was formed at Somerset House which later became the South Kensington School of Art. Stanhope Forbes studied at the Royal Academy under Leighton and Alma-Tadema in 1876. Little is known of how much they taught him; his interest in drawing had begun earlier at Dulwich College where he boarded and was taught by John Sparkes. Forbes followed Sparkes to Lambeth School of Art before entering the Academy; Sparkes later became head of the South Kensington School.

5
Old Newlyn Harbour c1880s (Penlee House Gallery and Museum, on loan from The Cornwall Centre)

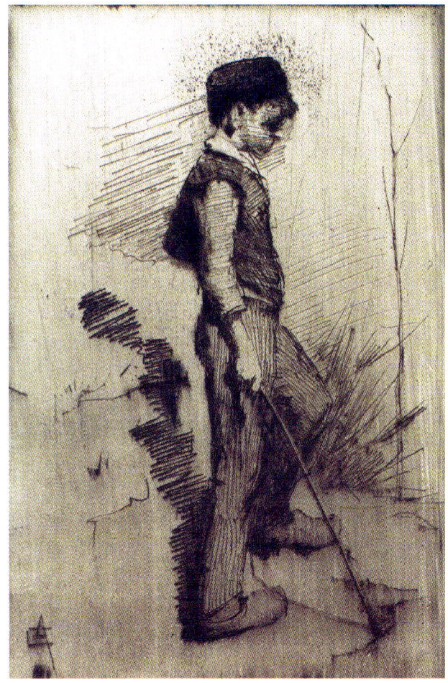

6
Elizabeth Forbes (née Armstrong) *Boy with a Stick* c1883 drypoint etching 10.1x7cm (Penlee House Gallery and Museum)

Walter Langley won a scholarship in 1873 to study at the South Kensington School where he was able to draw from the life model. This was still seen by teachers to be of little use in enabling an artist to earn a living, but it was of great significance to many of the Newlyn painters who went on to make complex figure paintings. In 1873, when she was just 14 years old, Canadian-born Elizabeth Armstrong travelled from America to the South Kensington School to study.

Many other Newlyners studied at the Slade School of Art, founded in 1871 as part of the University College London. It offered a more enlightened training compared to the Royal Academy and the South Kensington School. The Victorian classical influence was still present in the form of its first Professor, Edward Poynter, however, Poynter made drawing from the life model the core of his teaching. In 1875, Poynter resigned and was replaced by the French painter Alphonse Legros (1837–1911) who changed the emphasis in teaching to a more continental practice. He was also a master etcher and this art form was taught to artists such as Henry Scott Tuke who studied at the Slade from 1875–1880. Tuke was an early visitor to Newlyn in 1883 before he settled permanently in Falmouth in 1885. Other Slade-trained artists who came to Newlyn were Percy Craft (1856–1934), Albert Chevallier Tayler (1862–1925), Frank Wright Bourdillon (1851–1924), Thomas Cooper Gotch (1854–1931), and Arthur Bateman (1847–1894). Many of these artists made friendships at the Slade which they maintained for the rest of their lives. Other significant art schools were Heatherley's School of Art and Herkomer's School, also known as Bushey.

However, London art schools were only seen as the beginning of an art education at this time and the Slade offered scholarships for its students to study abroad in ateliers in Paris, Antwerp and Munich. Paris was regarded as the centre of art in Europe. The Newlyn painters either studied at the Académie Julian set up in 1873 by Rudolphe Julian, JP Laurens' studio or Leon Bonnat's. The studios gave students a basic knowledge of painting and drawing. The atmosphere in French studios was very different from the English. There was whistling and shouting and a more laid back attitude; friendships made at the London art schools and at the foreign ateliers were a significant factor in creating the Newlyn colony of artists.

It was the personality and reputation of the individual tutors in the ateliers, which was the main attraction for the students. Stanhope Forbes went to study at Leon Bonnat's studio in February 1880. Although Bonnat only visited the studio once a week, Forbes obviously felt he was the right tutor for him: 'With my particular faults in painting he is just the man.'[2] Bonnat's main influence on Forbes was his belief in observing nature very closely. He also used deep colours and painted with powerful brushwork. Thomas Gotch and Caroline Burland Yates (1854–1945) both studied at Julian's academy but Gotch preferred Laurens' studio. 'I like Laurens, he is very original in composition and interests himself in it. The noise, the heat, the smoke and the students generally, depress me beyond measure, and I am played out pretty soon every day, but one learns.'[13] Thomas Gotch had had an extensive art education by this time, including six months at Verlat's Studio in the Ecole des Beaux Arts, Antwerp. Verlat's was also popular with artists who were to come to Nelwyn including Edward Harris, Frank Bramley, Fred Hall (1860–1948) and Norman Garstin. A love of Dutch art remained with these artists and influenced their work.

It was whilst at Antwerp under Verlat that Frank Bramley formed the painting technique that was to become known as the 'square brush technique'. It was based on making a small quick sketch which showed the individual brushstrokes. The brushstrokes became even more heavily emphasized when using a square ended brush. This technique was taught in other ateliers in France and when back in England many of the Newlyn painters used this technique and as a group were defined by it. The idea behind the square brush technique was to free the artist from getting too involved in detail and outline. It allowed the artist to focus on tonal values, using the juxtaposition of minute and subtle differences in the shades of a colour. Stanhope Forbes was a noticeable exponent of the square brush technique, which did not just rely on the shape of the brush to dictate the paint surface but encouraged a more vigorous approach to painting which involved stabbing the paint on rather than gently guiding the brush. The square brush technique resulted in a picture that was half way between Realism and Impressionism. The latter involved brushwork that was much more broken up and fragmented. The irony is that Forbes and his colleagues in Newlyn made a stand against the principles of Impressionism and yet the square brush technique was perhaps closer to it than any other form of English painting.

It was not surprising therefore, that when the Newlyn painters exhibited their work at the Royal Academy in London in the early 1880s, they were initially criticised as being too influenced by foreign art thinking, being seen as positively 'French' in their style. This was due not only to the use of the square brush technique but to the influence of the French painter, Jules Bastien-Lepage.

Bastien-Lepage was at the height of his fame as a painter in Paris in the 1880s. He made Naturalism paramount for an artist, observing nature in the form of rural landscapes and people. In order to achieve 'reality', Bastien-Lepage advocated painting *en plein air*, meaning to paint outdoors. Ideally it meant the artists going to live amongst their subjects; if it was a rural subject they were to live in the villages and observe everything first hand. This was certainly one of the main reasons why so many artists who had studied in France came to Nelwyn to seek out and be part of a rural culture. Most of Bastien-Lepage's paintings were of the locals in his native village of Damvilliers in the Meuse region of France. Bastien-Lepage was a Social Realist; his depictions of the poverty and brutal nature of hard labour were painted to shock the middle classes. The critics recognized that Bastien-Lepage attracted either great condemnation or overt praise from the art-going public. Norman Garstin called Bastien-Lepage 'the greatest of our day — almost all his contemporaries have felt his power; many imitated him, no one surpassed him. His men and women breathe air not linseed oil.' Stanhope Forbes on the occasion of Bastien-Lepage's death in 1884 wrote, 'So the greatest artist of our age is dead.... His influence on all the young painters, already so great, will become more powerful than ever.' Bastien-Lepage's paintings, though not entirely flat, were made with expressive brushmarks, and were not Impressionist. His adherence to Realism set him up as a catalyst for those

7
Elizabeth Forbes (née Armstrong)
Peeling Onions
1884/5
drypoint etching
15x8.9cm
(Penlee House Gallery and Museum)

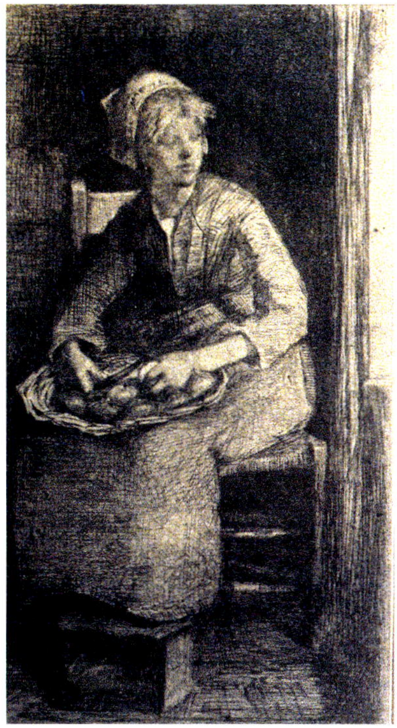

painters back in England who had rejected Impressionism for Realism such as Garstin, Forbes, and initially Tuke. Others, who embraced Impressionism, led by the American painter James McNeill Whistler (1834–1903) and Walter Sickert (1860–1942), felt that Bastien-Lepage's influence was holding back the development of painting in Britain and that Impressionism was the way forward. This difference of opinion was to manifest itself in a major walkout of Newlyn painters from the New English Art Club, which was set up in 1890 as an alternative to the Royal Academy.

The Parisian ateliers closed down in the summer and the painters headed for the northern coast of France, in particular Normandy and Brittany, where it was cooler and the light and water as well as the rural village people made it an ideal painting spot. The Bretons maintained many of their cultural traditions, festivals and religious ceremonies, which included wrestling and dancing as well as church services. They often wore their traditional costumes, which included complex headwear. Many of the foreign artists who went to paint in this region of France were also followers of Bastien-Lepage and his principles.

Stanhope Forbes first visited Brittany in 1881 with his old friend Henry La Thangue (1859–1929) who was studying at the Ecole des Beaux Arts in Paris when Forbes was at Bonnat's studio. They visited St Briac and then went on to Cancale where Forbes stayed until October. The aim of the trip was to paint outdoors directly from nature. The difference between principle and reality became starkly clear to Forbes. He did not find the Bretons charming but described them as 'a very dirty, uninteresting, drunken sort'.[4] He also soon learnt how difficult it was to paint outdoors, with the wind blowing his easel over, the sun kept moving and changing the light, the dust getting in his eyes and the problems with models. Despite all this he was to have his first success at the Royal Academy with a painting called *A Street in Brittany* (1881) painted at Cancale. It was bought by the Walker Art Gallery, Liverpool for their collection and Forbes later told the curator there that the purchase of the painting had encouraged him to pursue outdoor painting rather than the safer option of portraiture.

In the summer of 1882 Forbes returned to Brittany, this time venturing to the small town of Quimperlé, where he met Ralph Todd (1856–1932), William Blandford Fletcher (1858–1936) and Leghe Suthers (1855–1924): all later to come to Newlyn. In October 1883, Forbes arrived at Pont Aven, which had become the most popular Breton village for foreign artists to paint. Edwin Harris came to Pont Aven in the summer of 1882 after visiting Dinan with William Breakspeare (1856–1914) in 1881. Harris' biographer described the density of the artistic population in Brittany at the time: 'In those days there was hardly a village in Brittany which was not occupied by one or two painters. But at Pont Aven they simply

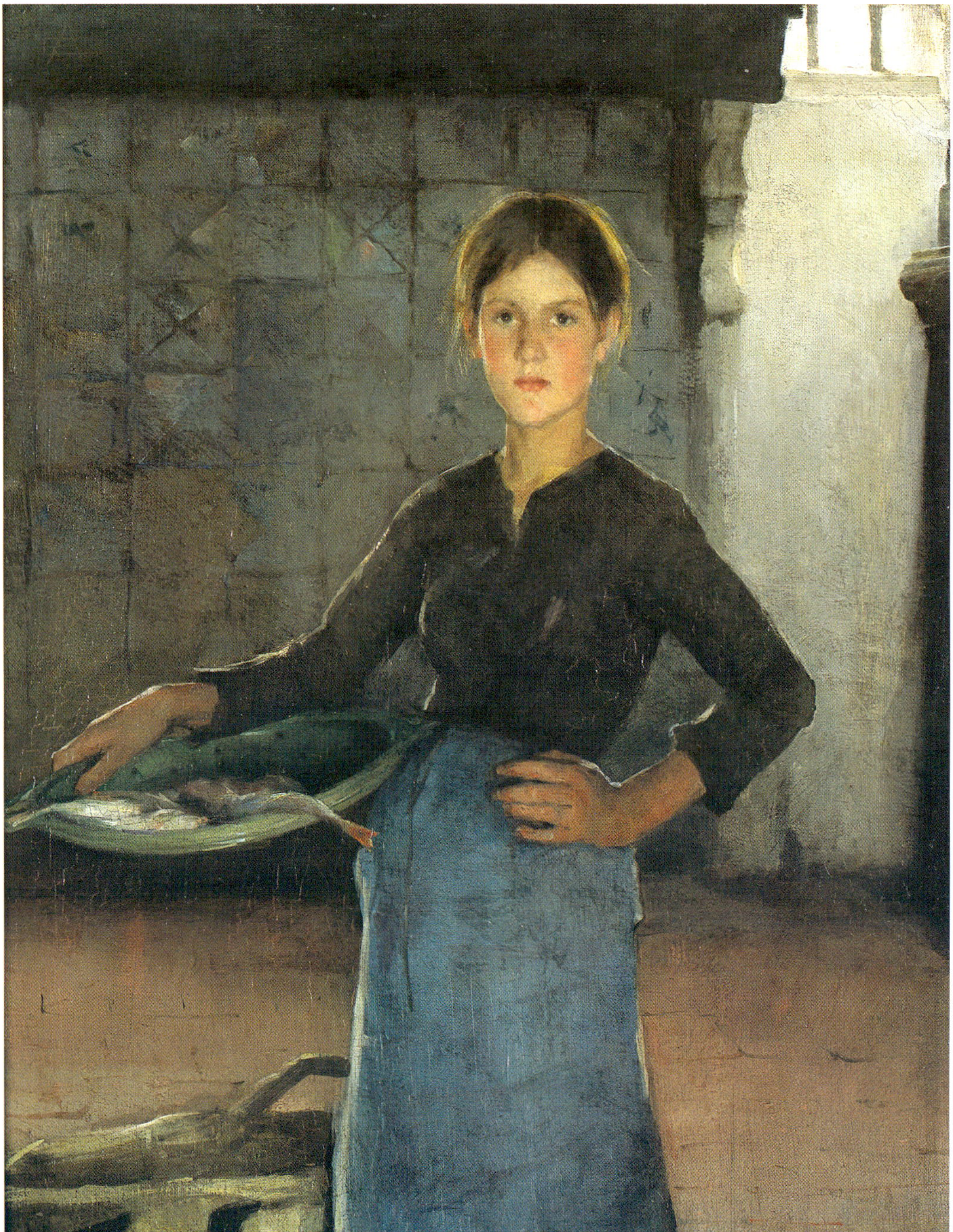

8
Elizabeth Forbes (née Armstrong)
A Zandvoort Fisher Girl 1884
oil on canvas
67.3x53.3cm
(Penlee House Gallery and Museum, on loan from Newlyn Art Gallery)

swarmed — English, French, Americans and representatives of almost all nationalities. This little village, shut in on all sides by the wooded hills, was then, and probably still is, a most unhealthy spot in which to make a lengthy habitation. It can boast none of the picturesque wooden architecture, which is so attractive in so many of the Breton towns, but the costume of the natives.... is probably the most picturesque in Finistère. Crowding its small hotel, and few inns, and overflowing into the one or two narrow streets. Some seventy or eighty painters, mostly quite young, were spending a happy life of hard work, intermingled with joyous recreation. Within the walls of the Hotel des Voyageurs, familiarly known as 'Julia's', after the landlady, a buxom dame whose reputation extended to every place where art jargon flourished in France were to be found representatives of all the 'schools' and movements of the day.'[5]

Elizabeth Armstrong went to Brittany in 1882 in the hope of finding greater encouragement from fellow artists than she had received previously in Munich where she had found her 'sex to be a perpetual disadvantage.' She had struggled with the teaching in Munich for five months before returning to London. Then after receiving news of the creative and companionable atmosphere of Pont Aven, Elizabeth made her way there with her mother. 'I cannot describe the charm of the impression this old Breton land...makes on me.'[6] Whilst in Pont Aven, Elizabeth made her first exhibited works, mainly watercolours. She gave herself the challenge of painting the local children — they were possibly the most troublesome models. She once made the mistake of feeding one of the village urchins who later installed himself with his friend in her studio for three days before she had to ask Madame Julia from the Hotel des Voyageurs to come and dislodge them.

In 1884, after her return to London, Elizabeth Armstrong persuaded her uncle to allow her to go to Holland so she could work with her old tutor from New York, William Chase at Zandvoort, near Haarlem. One of her most important paintings from this period is *A Zandvoort Fisher Girl* (1884) (Penlee). Children both at work and play were to become her main subject in forthcoming years. On her return to London in late 1884 after the summer in Holland, she began studying drypoint etching under Walter Sickert and James McNeill Whistler. Whistler had developed the practice of etching as an art form in its own right. She used the sketches she had made in Zandvoort as the basis for her etchings. She became very successful in this medium and was invited to become a member of the Royal Society of Painter Etchers. Good examples of Elizabeth Armstrong's etchings from this period are *Peeling Onions* (1884/5) (Penlee) and *Boy with a Stick* (c1883) (Penlee).

Norman Garstin's (1847–1926) *Among the Pots* (Plymouth) and *Church of St Michèle, Quimperlé* (Plymouth) of about 1882 are examples of work from these years. Garstin had studied at Antwerp at Verlat's Academy in 1878 along with Frank Bramley and Fred Hall. Both these paintings reflect the more sombre colours of his northern training. However, Garstin then went to Paris in 1880 and studied at Carolus Duran's atelier. He met Degas and went to the main Impressionist exhibitions held at the time. He was a admirer of Manet and was impressed by the brightness of his work which influenced Garstin later on in his career.

Describing the attractions for the artists who painted in the art colonies of Pont Aven, Quimperlé and Zandvoort goes some way to explaining why so many of the English-based artists, when they had finished their studies in the ateliers, returned home to find an equivalent to these rural idylls. Newlyn in Cornwall had many parallels with the villages of Pont Aven and Quimperlé.

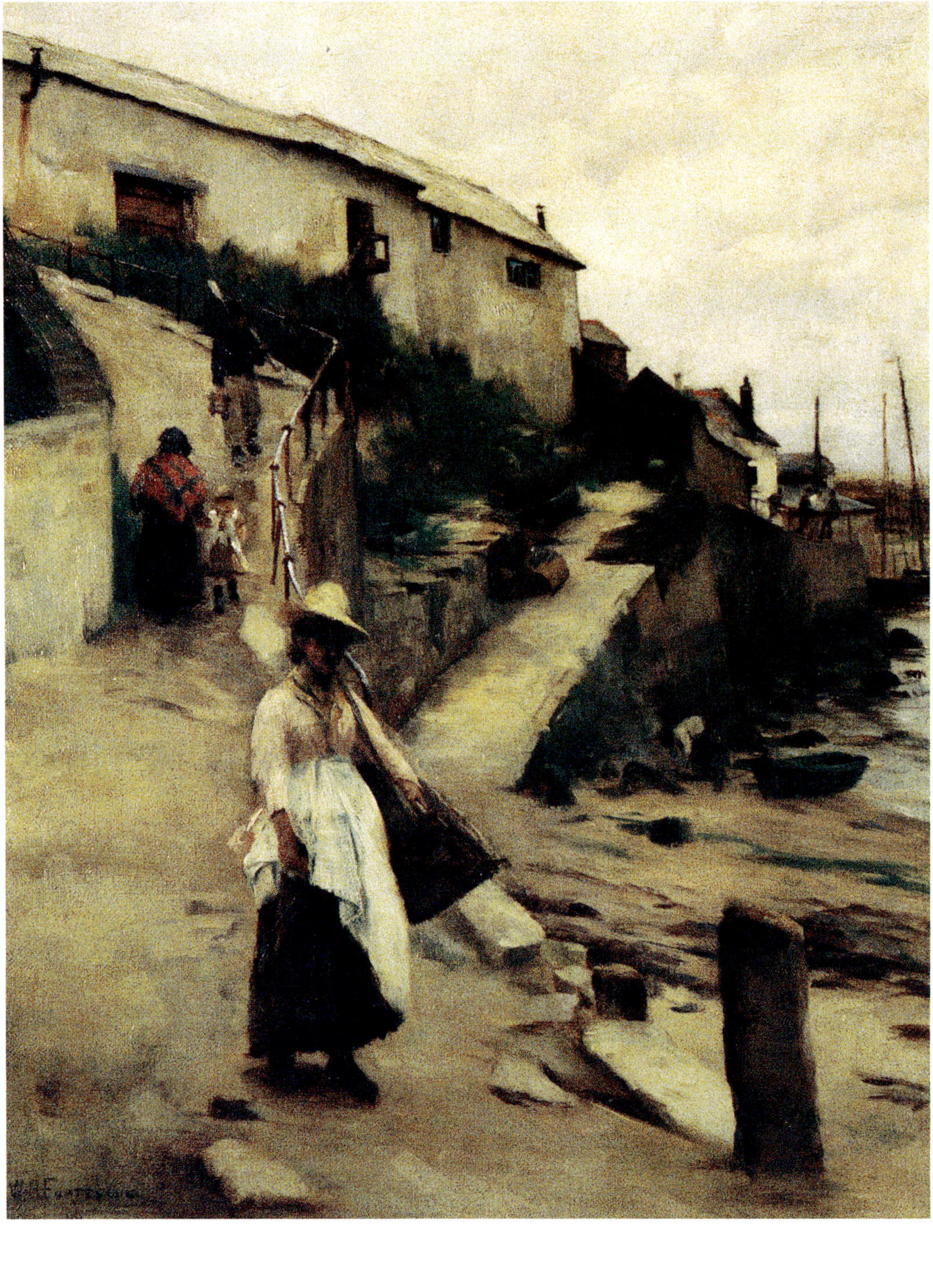

9
William Banks Fortescue
Newlyn Old Harbour 1891
oil on canvas
37x30cm
(Penlee House Gallery and Museum)

10
Frederick James McNamara Evans
Old Fisherman
date unknown
watercolour
20.3x14.5cm
(Penlee House Gallery and Museum)

2 Life in Newlyn - Fish and Art

What was the attraction of Newlyn? It was certainly picturesque. The 'Newlyn Town' clung to the side of a steep hill on the west side of the Coombe river which in the 1880s divided it from the rest of the village known as Street-an-Nowan. At this time the beach was all that connected the two; the Slip, down to the beach, became the traditional boundary between the two villages. The cobbled streets were linked through a maze of narrow lanes called 'opes' leading into courtyards on different levels with no particular overall plan.

Though undeniably picturesque Newlyn would not have been the focus for so many artists had it not in part replicated the culture and environment they had experienced in Brittany. The Bretons and the Cornish shared many traditions, language and a similar landscape.

Before the railway link in 1852 the journey to Cornwall was tedious and long; initially artists painted rural views of Cornwall. Paintings of Kynance Cove in particular were shown at the Royal Academy and the Royal Watercolour Society in the 1870s. It was probably seeing these works that gave the Birmingham-based artist Walter Langley the idea to pay a trip to Cornwall in 1880 to paint.

But it was the people, the fishermen and their wives who were the focus of the Newlyn painters for the first 20 years of the colony. The villagers' lives were hard and every aspect was dominated by the sea and the fishing industry. The census of 1881 for the Parish of Paul recorded 6,005 people living in Newlyn and Mousehole and most were dependent on the fishing industry. The men worked out at sea on sailing boats, known as West Cornwall Luggers, which were used for catching mackerel and herring. There were no definable seasons for this, but they usually caught mackerel in the winter, in the spring drift nets were used far out into the Atlantic and then in the summer the fleet went in search of herring. The trips would be long; sometimes the men were gone for three months following the shoals of herring around the coast. They worked in the most basic conditions, there were no toilets and cooking facilities were very rudimentary. This made fishermen at the time 'as hard as their native granite.'[7] Pilchards were caught by the seine boats, with between six and eight rowers, working in threes with a large net.

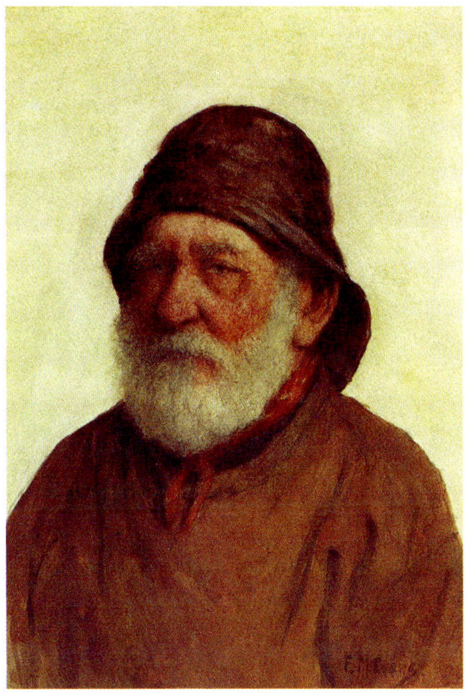

The women's work was equally tough, wet, cold and exhausting, working on the quayside or in the cellars gutting, packing and salting. Some fish was sold locally. 'A jouster (a hawker of fish) would cover up to nine parishes which would take the whole day to complete on foot, carrying a burden of close on a hundredweight; comprising about 40lbs of salt in large pockets around her waist and the rest in a cowal or basket on her back.'[8] It was up to them to collect the fish in baskets on their backs from the various places where the fisherman had brought the catch to shore. These were sold by auction to fish 'hawkers' or 'jousters'. Walter Langley's *Breadwinners* (1896) (Penlee) which he did both as an oil and as a watercolour, shows women collecting and carrying fish in the cowals on their backs, trudging their weary way along the beach. The poverty in Newlyn was as real as that in the industrial cities but it was set against an idyllic landscape and even though the early artists were Social Realists they tended to romanticize working life.

Of course a fishing village had one inevitable drawback. 'Several times I have been shocked and disgusted with the state of the thoroughfares, mud and filth and rotten fish lying about and trampled underfoot. And then the smells! In certain conditions of the atmosphere the effluvia are something appalling and anyone with a delicate olfactory apparatus would barely survive the stinks and stenches which rise sometimes to pollute the live air. But the inhabitants go about their business or their pleasure with a stoic indifference for such trifles and might be furnished with wooden noses for all it affects them.'[9] Perhaps the artists became as stoical or indifferent to the stench as the inhabitants.

11
Stanhope Forbes painting in Boase Street, Newlyn (Penlee House Gallery and Museum, on loan from The Cornwall Centre)

12
Walter Langley *Breadwinners* c1896 watercolour 23x43cm (Penlee House Gallery and Museum)

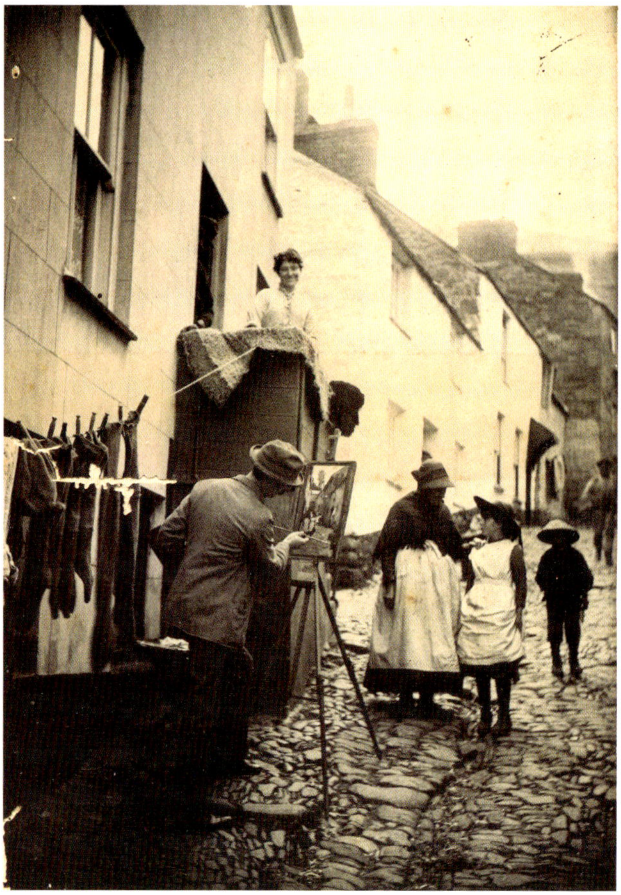

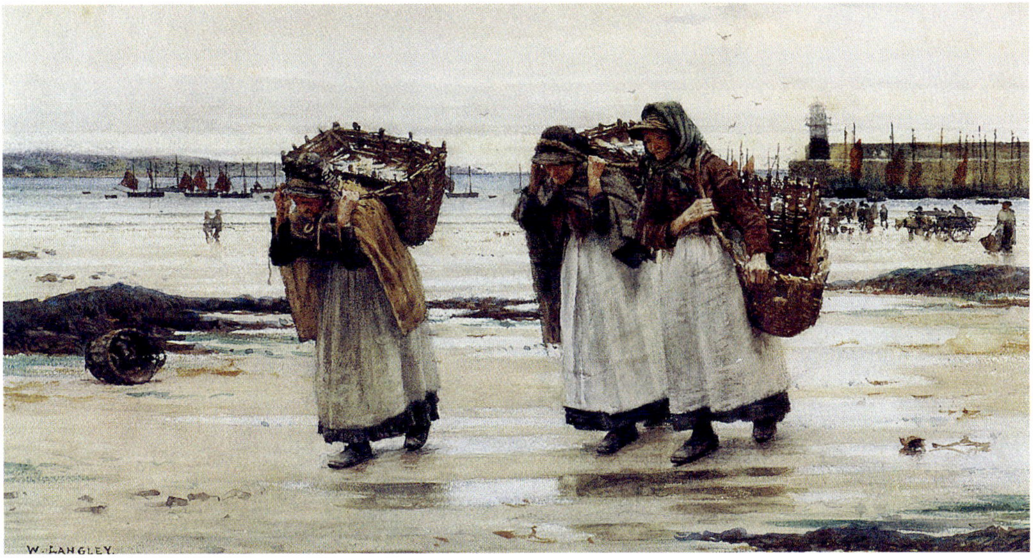

Walter Langley (1852–1922)

Walter Langley lived and worked in Birmingham for thirty years before he came to Newlyn. He trained as a designer at the South Kensington School, painting as a hobby. He returned to Birmingham to become a partner in a firm of lithographers, Biermanns, where he had served his apprenticeship. Painting was so important to him that he enrolled in evening classes at Birmingham Society of Arts to improve his painting skills in the figure and costume classes; he also studied alternate evenings at Birmingham School of Design. After his marriage to Clara Perkins and the birth of their first son Lorraine in 1877, Langley dramatically increased the number of paintings he made; he began to record their sales. In 1879, his first year as a professional artist, he sold 66 paintings but only earned £288; the highest price he received for a work that year was £19.

Langley's first sketching trips to Newlyn were in 1880 and later for a month in 1881. For the first half of his career he was watercolourist, which makes him unusual amongst the Newlyn painters. He was not an outdoor painter as such; he drew sketches on the spot, then took them back to his studio to make larger pictures. His interiors and figures were not painted directly from life, but the details could only have come from hours of accurate observation. Painting models from life was a more challenging business and cost money; Langley also bought costumes for models to wear which ate into his meagre income.

In March 1882 Langley moved to Cornwall permanently when he was offered £500 for a year's work in Newlyn through his agent JW Thrupp, a Birmingham photographer and art dealer. He also had a commission for twenty paintings from Edwin Chamberlain, a Birmingham gallery owner. The Thrupp commission allowed Langley to rent a house, Pembroke Lodge, not far from Newlyn harbour with a studio in the garden. He also rented a studio in the village for the convenience of his models.

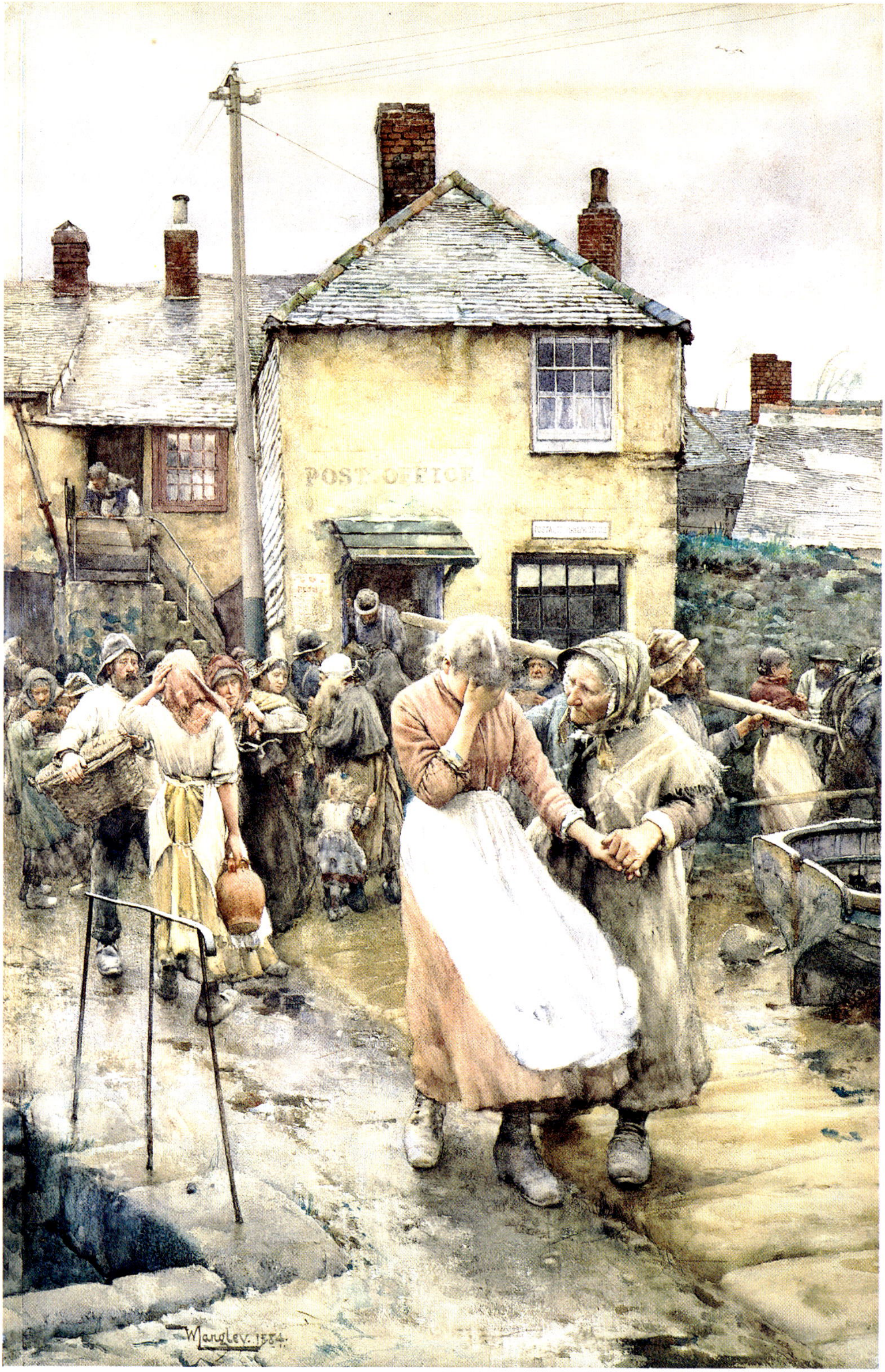
POST OFFICE
Langley. 1884.

13
Walter Langley
Among the Missing — Scene in a Cornish Fishing Village 1884
watercolour
103x70cm
(Penlee House Gallery and Museum)

14
Photo of
Walter Langley
(Shears Fine Art)

15
Walter Langley
In a Cornish Fishing Village — Departure of the Fleet for the North
1886 watercolour
61x122cm
(Penlee House Gallery and Museum)

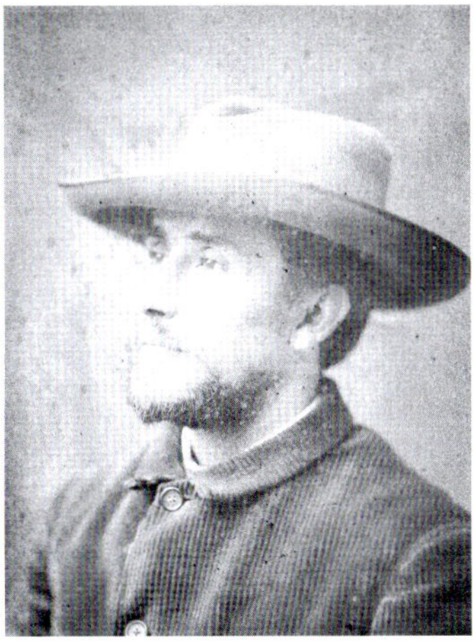

Langley's depictions of the people of Newlyn are social comments on the poverty and hardship of their lives, emphasised by the moral and complex titles he gave them. His paintings were often of women, young and old, who were left at home to work and worry about their men at sea. Langley portrays the anxiety of these women through their poses which frequently involve the grieving woman with her head bent and her face covered by her hand. She is usually a young woman accompanied by a much older woman who is there to comfort her, for example *For men must work and women must weep, Though storms be sudden and waters deep, And the harbour bar be moaning,* (1882) (Birmingham Museums and Art Gallery) and *Among the Missing – Scene in a Cornish Fishing Village* (1884) (Penlee).

For men must work and women must weep, has an air of tranquillity about it, whereas *Among the Missing,* communicates more of the panic and dumbstruck shock of hearing bad news and the affect on a tightly knit community. Other 'action' paintings by Langley include *Disaster* (1889) (Birmingham Museums and Art Gallery). The only painting where Langley depicted an actual dead body was in *After the Storm* (1894) (Birmingham Museums and Art Gallery). In his major watercolour *In a Cornish Fishing Village — Departure of the Fleet for the North* (1886) (Penlee) Langley uses a long narrow format for his composition – a device he used many times, which reflects the panoramic nature of the sea view. The ships on the horizon are the subject of this painting, but are used by Langley as a backdrop for a complex figure composition in the foreground.

Langley gained recognition for these paintings in the 1890s but only after he had painted a major work in oil. *Among the Missing* won a gold medal at the Paris Salon and so did *The Departure of the Fleet* in Chicago. In 1897, an article was written about Langley in 'The Moseley and King's Heath Journal', which sums up what Langley was trying to achieve in his paintings. 'His interest, he remarked, has always been with the workers and toilers; and although not what may be termed a pessimist, he is forever impressed by the signs of the

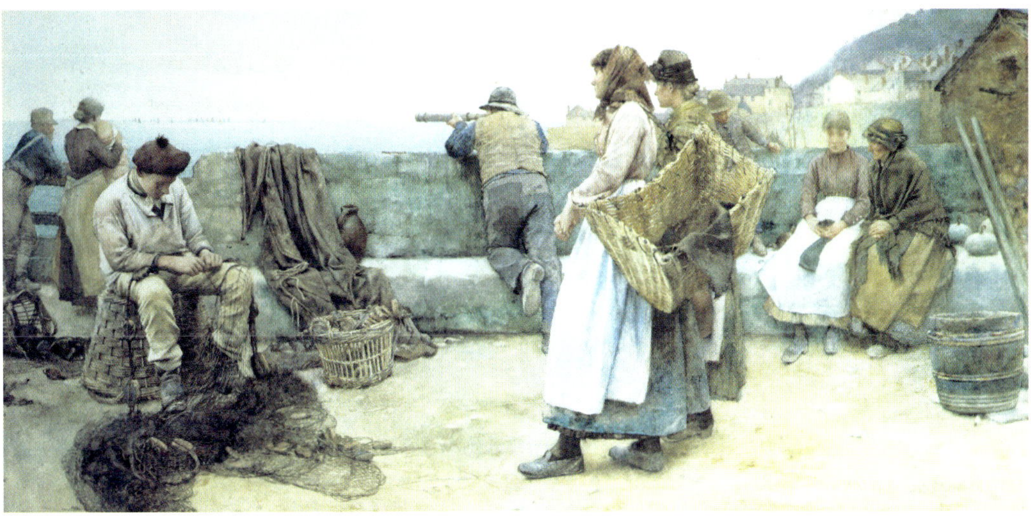

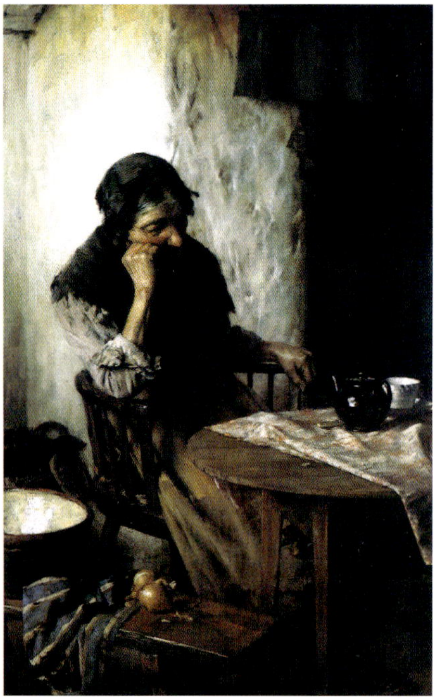

struggle for existence which are so apparent throughout nature, and which entails here and there so much misery and pain.'

Langley's *When One is Old* (1895) (Plymouth) is one of many paintings of old Newlyn fisherwomen sitting with only their memories to keep them company. The woman is shown with one arm on the chair and the chin resting on her hand and knuckles, the eyes staring at nothing in particular. There is great sense of resigned sadness in the down-turned mouth but there is also a determination in the lines around the mouth signifying the pain and suffering that have been endured.

16
Walter Langley
When One is Old
1895
oil on canvas
70x45.7cm
(Plymouth City Museum and Art Gallery)

17
Walter Langley
The Sunny South
1885
oil on canvas
122x61cm
(Penlee House Gallery and Museum)

The Sunny South (1885) (Penlee) is a typical Cornish pastoral scene but rare for Langley. This painting was set in the garden at Pembroke Lodge. It is an unusually tall format, which allows Langley to show the view of Newlyn and the sea beyond. This early oil demonstrates his desire to reach the same standards in this medium as in his familiar watercolours.

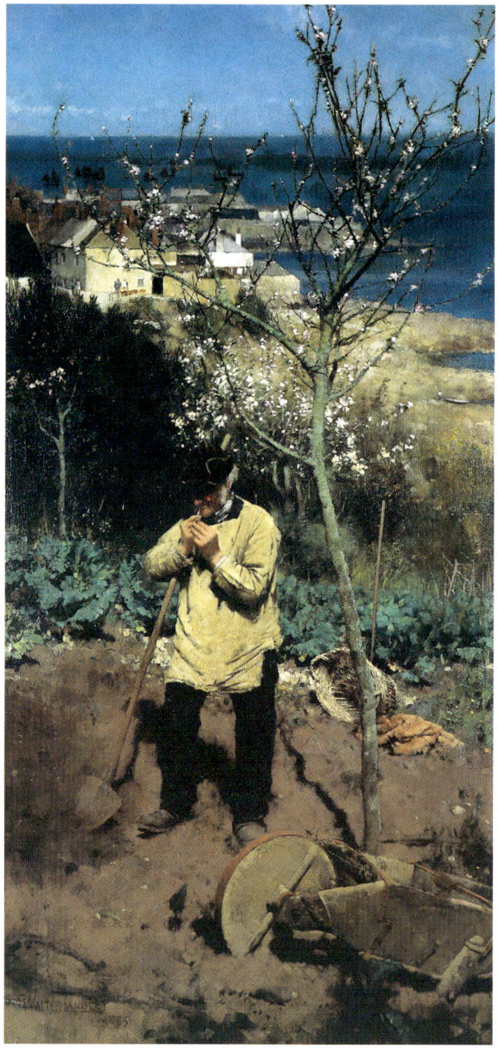

18
Edwin Harris
The Lesson 1889
oil on canvas
51x60cm
(Penlee House Gallery and Museum, on loan from Private Collection)

19
Edwin Harris
Old Fisherwoman
date unknown
oil on canvas
19x14.7
(Penlee House Gallery and Museum)

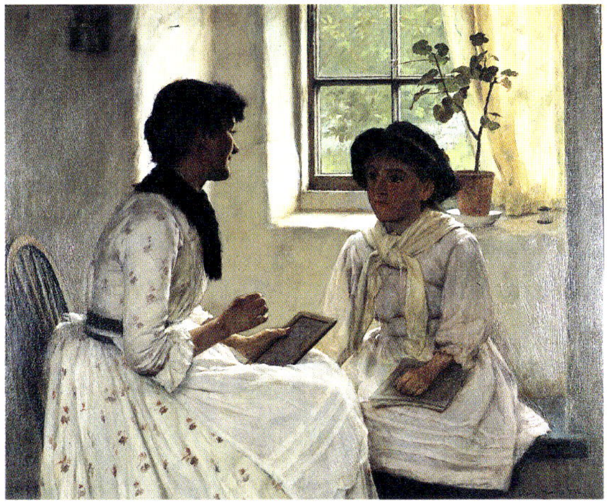

Edwin Harris (1855–1906)

Edwin Harris and his wife were very hospitable; Forbes described the pleasant times they had: 'Thursday, I dined with the Harrises and met little Bateman and his wife. Wonderful dinner, beginning with ducks and ending with a joint. After dinner, music. Little Bateman plays the flute beautifully. When they had departed Langley sat down, played dance music and we had a little dance – quadrilles, waltzes, polkas etc. Mrs Harris pronouncing me quite a good dancer.'[10] (Little Bateman refers to Arthur Bateman an artist and entrepreneur who came from London.) On the occasion of Langley leaving Newlyn temporarily in 1886, the artists had a party at Bellevue. They left at 2.00am in the morning processing through the streets with Langley playing his banjo and singing 'as we went home by the light of the moon.'[11]

Harris was a master of portraiture and his painting *Old Fisherwoman* (date unknown) (Penlee) has all the cares and troubles of the hard life of a working fishwife depicted in the lines of this woman's face. It also shows what a master of depicting light he was, with the old woman's face strongly lit from one side setting up a wonderful profile allowing Harris to capture every detail and contour of her face.

Edwin Harris was best known for his depictions of interiors, particularly with women sitting on a window seat. *The Lesson* (1889) (Penlee) is a particularly good example of this. In it we see a woman, his regular model Kate Jeffreys, seated with a slate on her lap opposite a child on the window seat holding a book on her lap. The painting is a study in white with the woman's white dress broken only by a small pink floral pattern against the white cottage wall and the girl dressed in white. The power of the painting is in the connection between the two people, conveying a humanity and warmth of feeling between teacher and pupil.

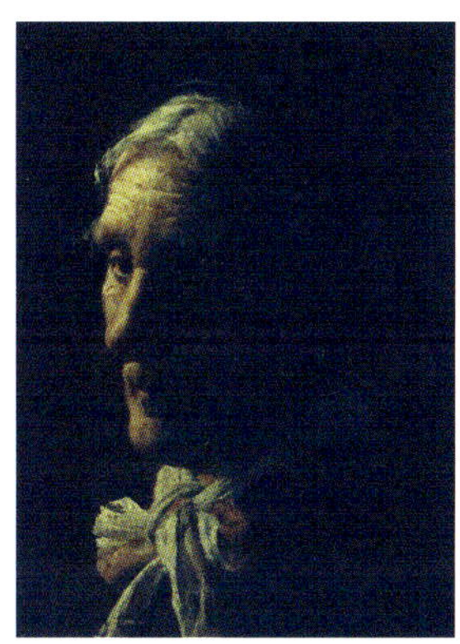

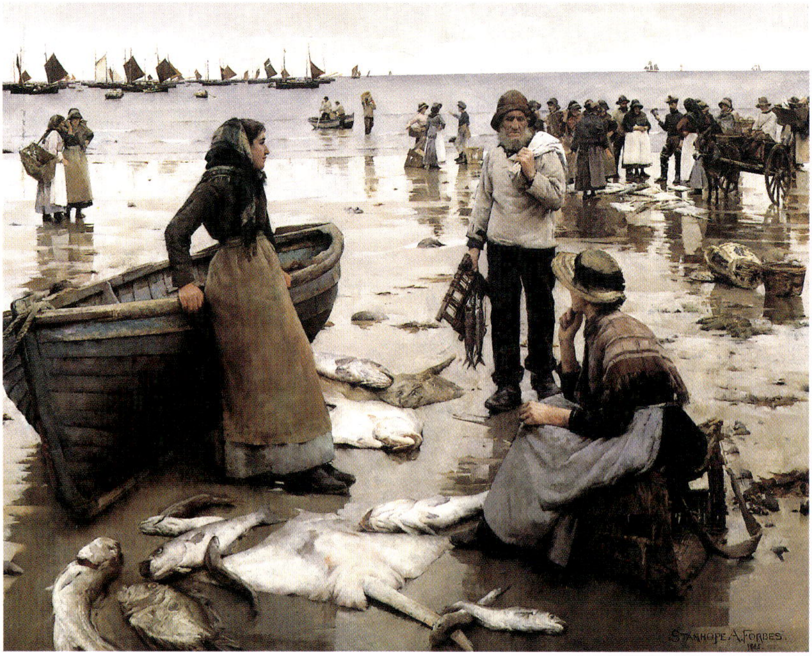

20
Alexander Stanhope Forbes, 1857-1947
Fish Sale on a Cornish Beach
1885
oil on canvas
121.5x155cm
(Plymouth City Museum and Art Gallery)
© Courtesy of the artist's estate/ Bridgeman Art Library

Stanhope Alexander Forbes (1857–1947)

Stanhope Forbes was attracted to Newlyn to paint the fishermen and women. He focussed on more positive images rather than dwelling on the morbid or dramatic stories as described in Langley's paintings. One of the other marked differences between Forbes and Langley's work was that Forbes applied the principles of the French painter Bastien-Lepage. Forbes' pictures can be seen more as a celebration of the fishing people's lives, romanticizing their existence and dwelling on the picturesque quality of the village and its surrounding countryside, avoiding moral messages on the plight of the working class.

Forbes came to Cornwall in January 1884 when he took a train to Falmouth. He considered settling in Porthleven but Newlyn was the place he fell in love with. He had just returned from painting on the Breton coast of France so it is hardly surprising that he described Newlyn as 'a sort of English Concarneau'. The paintings he had done in France were not selling well in London and he 'decided that subjects from nearer home might have a greater appeal.'[12]

The painting that made Forbes' name in London and which heralded him as the star of the Newlyn School was *Fish Sale on a Cornish Beach* (1885) (Plymouth). It was a large canvas, 121.5x155cm and took a year to complete. Although mainly a figure composition, the inspiration for the picture was obviously the colours and reflections found on the beach at low tide. Forbes wrote to his mother, 'Anything more beautiful than this beach at low water I never saw and if I can only paint figures against such a background as this shining mirror-like shore makes, the result should be effective.'

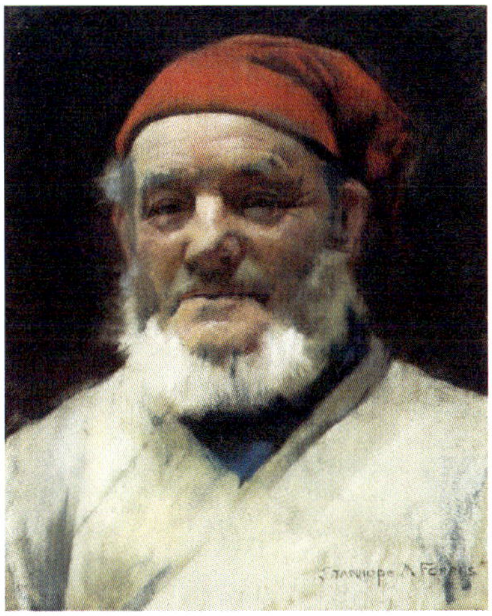

21
Alexander Stanhope Forbes, 1857-1947 *Old Martin Sampson* date unknown pastel on canvas 29.3x24.2cm (Plymouth City Museum and Art Gallery) © Courtesy of the artist's estate/ Bridgeman Art Library

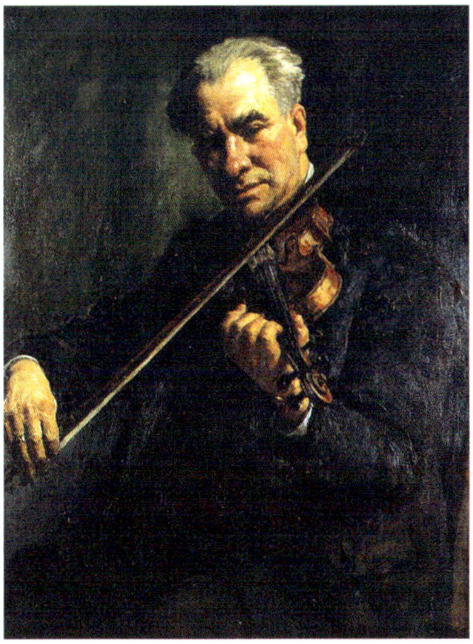

22
Alexander Stanhope Forbes, 1957-1947 *The Violinist (Walter Barnes)* date unknown oil on canvas 92x71.5cm (Penlee House Gallery and Museum, on loan from Penzance Orchestral Society) © Courtesy of the artist's estate/ Bridgeman Art Library

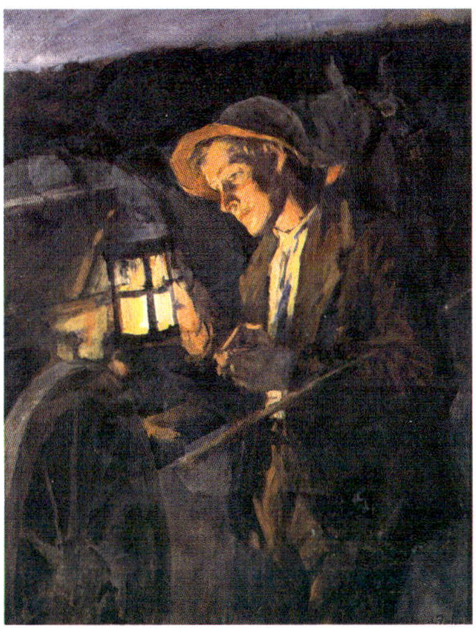

23
Alexander Stanhope Forbes, 1857-1947 *The Lighting Up Time* study 1901 oil on canvas 73x60cm (Royal Cornwall Museum, Truro) © Courtesy of the artist's estate/ Bridgeman Art Library

1885 was a particularly good year for fishing in Newlyn and sales of fish on the beach were a regular occurrence. Stanhope Forbes wrote at the time, 'never has there been such fishing known, and were it not that fish are so cheap the people would all be rolling in money. Boats are bringing in as many as 12,000 mackerel and the great difficulty is to find means of packing these large quantities. The salesmen's bell is heard each minute, and the beach is always crowded with buyers.'[13]

It cannot have been easy for Forbes to paint this picture. He could only go out when the sky was overcast and the tide was out. He had to face the elements of wind and rain and so did his models who, from his accounts, were posing outside on the beach for him. He wrote that one of them fainted in the appalling conditions. He always worked directly from life in all weathers. 'I have never painted with such directness as on those fortunately rare occasions when I worked at sea, and I have carried large pictures right through to the last touch in smithies, stables, sheds, and amid all sorts of queer conditions which when starting seemed absolutely hopeless and prohibitive. It is much discussed whether it is better to work directly from nature or to make innumerable studies or notes and paint the picture from them I believe no rule can be laid down, and that it is entirely a matter of individual temperament. My own custom has been to work as much as possible on the spot, and practice has taught me that this offers certain advantages over any other method. There is a quality of freshness most difficult of attainment by any other course, and which one is too apt to lose when the work is brought into the studio for completion.'[14] *Fish Sale* was painted on a dull overcast day, a trait that became a regular feature in Newlyn School paintings, which acts as a way of emphasizing the light in the picture. In this case the light emanates from the white bellies of the fish and the reflections of sky and sea in the pools on the beach.

At one point, in October, he thought he would not finish the painting in time for the Royal Academy but with encouragement from his fellow painters Tuke and Chevallier Tayler he did manage to complete this as well as another painting. The

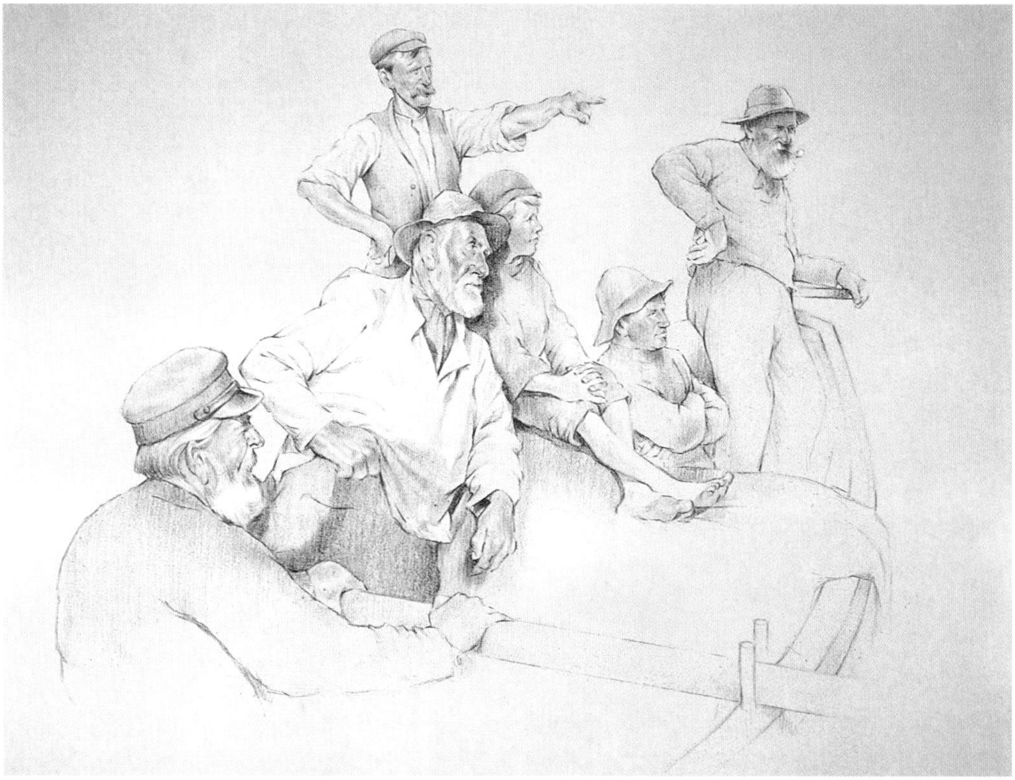

painting is a very cleverly balanced composition. It was highly acclaimed by the critics when it appeared in the Royal Academy in 1885, but the Chantrey Bequest refused to purchase it for the nation for being 'too positively the outcome of a foreign school.' Instead it was sold at Dowdeswells of Bond Street for 250 guineas.

Alice Meynell, an art critic, wrote one of the first articles highlighting the significance of the Newlyn School for 'The Art Journal' in 1889. In it she announced that Forbes' *Fish Sale* 'manifests the finest quality of natural Art. It is a triumph of pictorial vision.'[15] Meynell recognized that Forbes was mainly interested in painting light and it was this which gave *Fish Sale* 'its beautiful reality.' She goes on to praise the painting's 'distance, the measurable remoteness of the quiet horizon, the perspective of shore and sea, every hand's breadth of which has its own place; the lovely tints of the fish, the distinct and familiar humanity of each of the figures.'[16] It was very hard for Forbes to follow up the overwhelming success of this picture. Initially, his submission for the Royal Academy in 1886 *Off to the Fishing Grounds*, (Walker Art Gallery) did not receive anywhere near the same acclaim.

Stanhope Forbes was fortunate to find lodgings at Mrs Maddern's house Bellevue. Many of the artists who were central to the colony stayed here with Forbes at some point. In 1884 Forbes was joined by Chevallier Tayler and Blandford Fletcher and in 1886 by Frank Bourdillon, an artist who was also Forbes' fishing companion. Forbes' arrival seemed to initiate the social life for the Newlyn painters, as they all knew him socially as well as artistically. Although sometimes judgmental of his fellow artists, Forbes supported and encouraged them in their work. His frequent letters to his mother, with whom he had a very

24
Alexander Stanhope Forbes, 1857-1947
The Seine Boat study pencil drawing
(Royal Cornwall Museum, Truro)

25
Alexander Stanhope Forbes 1857-1947
Against Regatta Day c1905
oil on canvas
(Royal Cornwall Museum, Truro)

close relationship even after his marriage to Elizabeth Armstrong, are testament to this. Forbes described Blandford Fletcher as 'the best comrade I know.'[17] He also got on well with another lesser-known artist, Frank Bodilly (1860–?1926), who was a Cornishman and painted for two years before practising law. Forbes described him in his letters to his mother as 'Such a nice hearty fellow', 'a keen fisherman' and 'an amusing companion'.

Forbes continued his depiction of the Newlyners indoors in his major interiors of the 1880s. His interest in things musical was reflected in his major oil of 1888, *The Village Philharmonic* (Birmingham City Museums and Art Gallery). Set in a dark, gloomy room with the natural light coming from one small window and two lamps giving out a yellow glow, the painting is a study in light. *The Violinist* (date unknown) (Penlee) is a fine portrait of Walter Barnes who was the conductor of the Penzance Orchestral Society. The depiction of musicians was a popular theme amongst the Newlyn artists. His large interior paintings of the 1880s and 1890s included very detailed portraits of the local men and women who dominated these paintings, such as in *The Health of the Bride* (1889) (Tate Gallery) and *By Order of the Court* (1890) (Walker Art Gallery). One of his most detailed series of portraits of fishermen is in his painting *The Seine Boat* (1904) (Private Collection). The delicate pencil and chalk study for this painting, shows how Forbes drew each face from young lad to old hand with great precision and care. The picture featured Uncle William (second from the left) who was one of Forbes' favourite models, 'not only by reason of his fine physique, but also because of his frequent association with a nature so direct and true, so full of self-respecting dignity and affectionate fidelity, had brought about relationship between them more intimate than is common between artist and model'.[18] Uncle William appeared in several other paintings by Forbes including *Goodbye —Off to Skibbereen* (1901) (Private Collection), *The Fisherman's Yarn* (date and whereabouts unknown) and *The 22nd January 1901* (1901) (Royal Albert Memorial Museum, Exeter).

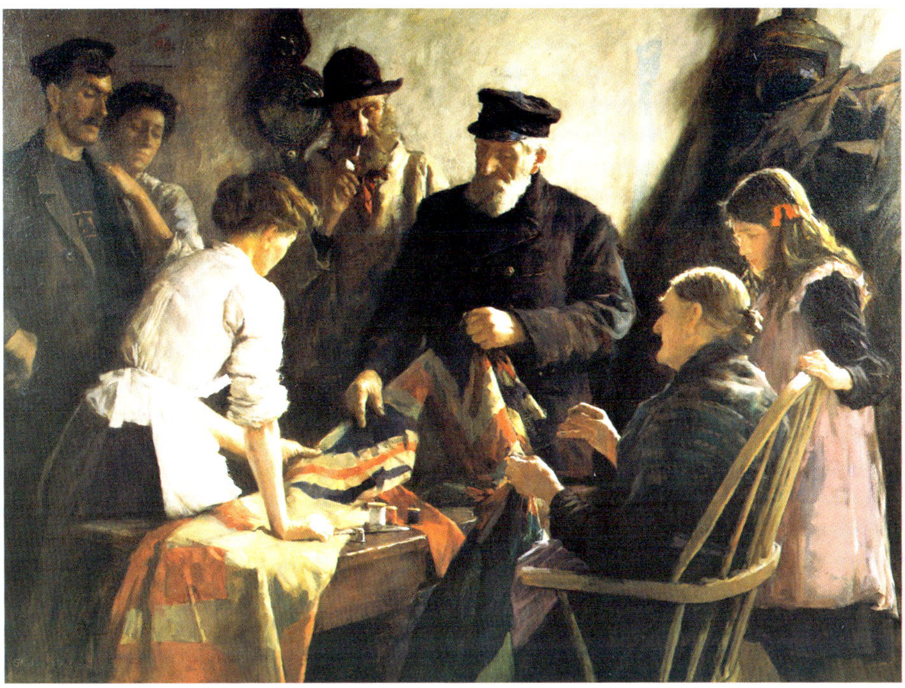

He gave up his rooms at Bellevue in 1889 and moved to Cliff Castle, owned by his new wife Elizabeth Armstrong's mother — the sale of *The Health of the Bride* in 1889 to Henry Tate had made it finally possible for the painter couple to marry. Elizabeth and Stanhope Forbes remained in Newlyn after their marriage; on the birth of their son Alec they moved to Trewarveneth (the House on the Hill) in 1893 and later in 1904–5 to Higher Faugan, which was even further into the countryside. Moving from the village led to both artists turning to more pastoral themes.

Forbes continued to depict working people but in different industries such as the quarrying of granite in *The Quarry Team* (1894) (Private Collection). This painting shows four great cart horses pulling a wooden wagon laden with one huge piece of granite set against a storm-ridden sky. It was painted the on the roadside near Sheffield's quarry. Forbes continued to paint rural interiors on the spot including *Forging the Anchor* (1892) (Ipswich Museums and Art Galleries) set in a blacksmith's. This became a favoured subject as he repeated it in a painting called *The Smithy* (date and whereabouts unknown). Forbes was possibly inspired by Henry Scott Tuke's *The Message* (1890) (Falmouth), as a subject for his major work *The Letter* (1898) (Plymouth). As in Tuke's painting, Forbes shows a woman reading a letter with her children whilst the postman stands by. The difference here is that Forbes has chosen the doorway rather than the interior of a rural cottage as his setting. It again gives Forbes the opportunity to use two minimal light sources to illuminate the characters in the painting, one being from the inside of the cottage, hidden from view, the other from the lamp hanging around the postman's neck. *The Lighting Up Time* (1901) (Royal Cornwall Museum) is another example of Forbes' fascination with, and ability to capture, low light levels either at dusk or dawn, or in dimly lit interiors. Placed in a rural setting, it is a painting of a mother with her baby asleep in her arms sitting in a cart in the foreground, with another young girl leaning over the side of the cart watching the young man light the lantern on the wagon. There is a herd of cattle being taken down the lane in the distance with farm buildings behind. The oil study for this painting focuses on the young man in the picture.

Forbes not only painted villagers at work, but also showed them enjoying their celebrations and festivals. *Against Regatta Day* (c1905) (Royal Cornwall Museum) is a typical example. Regattas were major events in the social calendars of all the fishing villages along the coast of Cornwall. Again Forbes shows his ability to capture the effect of light this time in a dark interior with light coming from a window at one side of the picture. He was always thinking about how tonal values of colours worked together. Forbes continued to paint his favourite Newlyn models in interiors, but from the turn of the century onwards, he concentrated on rural scenes where the small figures were dominated by the landscape, for example *Penolva* (1913) (Penlee). His earlier square brush technique of the 1880s was softened over the years and became much more impressionistic in his later work.

26
Thomas Cooper Gotch
Sharing Fish 1891
watercolour
(Royal Cornwall Museum, Truro)

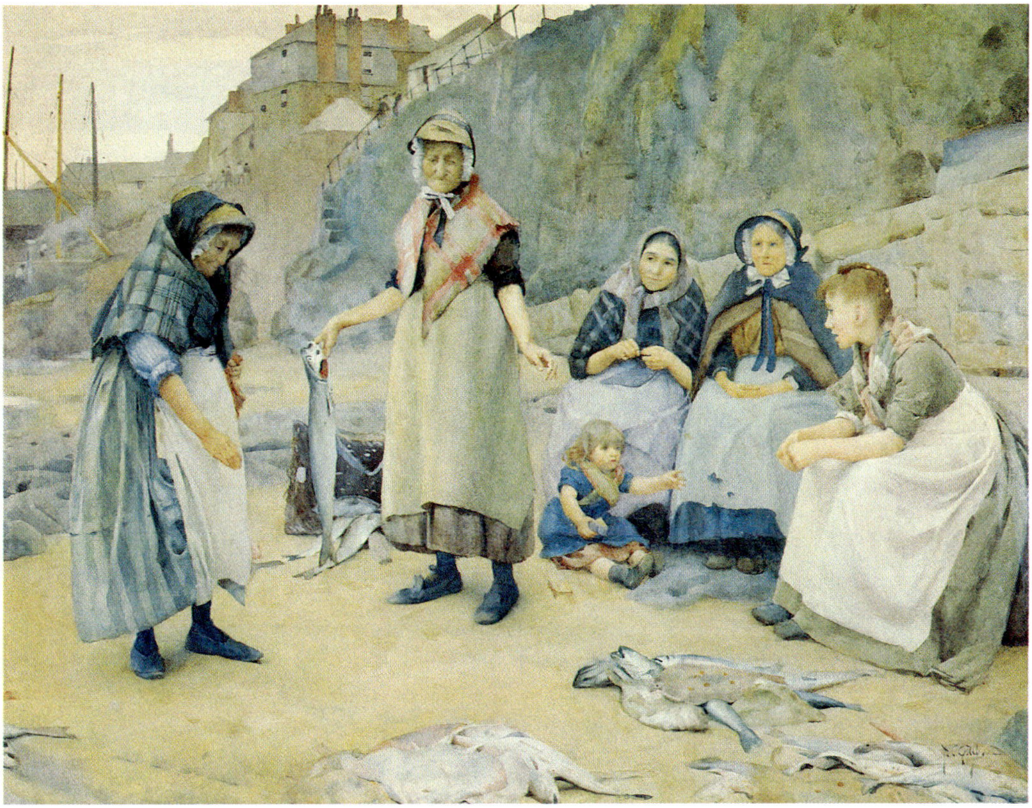

Thomas Cooper Gotch (1854–1931) and Caroline Burland Gotch (née Yates) (1854–1945)

Thomas Cooper Gotch also depicted the trials and tribulations of the Newlyn fisherfolk. He was not as consistent in this style as Langley or Forbes, but experimented with different approaches to painting. In 1891 Gotch completed *Sharing the Catch* (Private Collection). A watercolour version of this painting known as *Sharing Fish* (1891), is in the Royal Cornwall Museum's collection. The subject of these works is very similar to Forbes' *Fish Sale on a Cornish Beach*. Gotch's picture illustrates the village custom of the women, after sharing out the fish amongst themselves asking a passerby to check whether the catch is fairly divided. Instead of the sea as a backdrop, as in Forbes' painting, Gotch has placed the women in front of the Slip which was the steep walkway that lead down to the sea from the village. Gotch goes into far greater detail in the women's traditional costume in his painting than Forbes, and uses a much warmer palette of colour in his oil version. The watercolour is similar to the Forbes' oil painting as the dominant colour is blue. This painting is also significant in showing generations of women from the small child to the young woman, a well-known Newlyn model Mary Rowe, to the elderly woman sitting on the rocks. This portrayal of women through all the ages became a major theme in Gotch's work.

Gotch exhibited *The Heir to all the Ages* (whereabouts unknown) in 1897, which is completely different in subject and treatment. He had formed his interest in dressing his models up in elaborate gold brocaded costumes from a visit to Italy in the winter of 1891–1892 where he saw many renaissance paintings by Fra Angelico and Giovanni Bellini at the Uffizi in Florence. These artists were also the inspiration to the Pre-Raphaelites but Gotch was not a strict follower of their movement. Instead, he combined their principles of detail and truth to nature with more esoteric ideas of the Symbolist movement. He also brought into his pictures a love of Italian art, a love of the theatre, writing plays and poetry. The themes in many of his paintings were the stages of a woman's life from childhood to motherhood.

Gotch was also a great painter of children, especially young girls, with his daughter Phyllis featured as the main model. *Girl in a Cornish Garden* (1889) (Penlee) reflects both the child as an important subject but also Gotch's love of nature and painting landscapes. Although much of Gotch's later work was symbolic, using the figure as a metaphor, they were often placed in well observed natural surroundings which are clearly recognizable Cornish landscapes, such as *Madonna of the Mount* (1925–26) (The Alfred East Gallery, Kettering) and *The Flag* (1910) (The Alfred East Gallery, Kettering).

Gotch's wife Caroline was the youngest daughter of Edward Yates, a gentleman from Liverpool, much of whose wealth she later inherited. This gave her the independent means that a woman at that time needed in order to afford to study art. Caroline Yates came to Newlyn to paint as early as 1879 after studying at Heatherly's in 1878 and then going on to the Slade. This is where she first encountered Thomas Gotch as a fellow student. Gotch was at the time more interested in 'Bo' Santley and later became engaged briefly to his friend Henry Scott Tuke's sister, Maria. Tuke portrays 'Carrie', as she was known to her friends, in one of his earliest oil portraits *Portrait of Edith and Gertrude Santley with Carrie Yates* (1880) (York City Art Gallery).

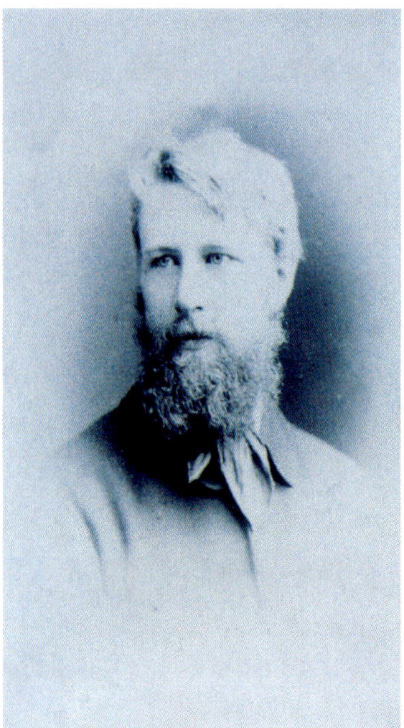

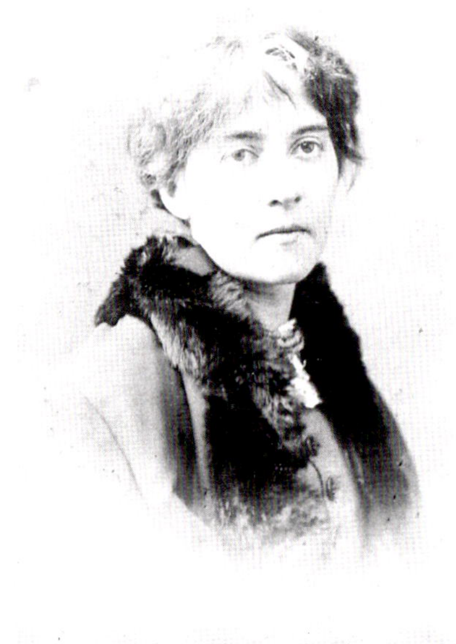

27
Photo of
Thomas Cooper
Gotch
(Shears Fine Art)

28
Photo of
Caroline Gotch
(Shears Fine Art)

29
Thomas Cooper
Gotch *Girl in a Cornish Garden*
1889
oil on canvas
30x22.5cm
(Penlee House
Gallery and
Museum, on loan
from a Private
Collection)

After a short time in Newlyn Caroline Yates went to Laurens' atelier in Paris where her friendship with Gotch blossomed. They were married in August 1881 in Newlyn, before returning to Paris to continue their studies. Caroline Gotch had their one and only child, Phyllis, on 6th September 1882 in Brolles. She suffered from ill health immediately after the birth and for many years was in and out of hospitals. Despite this, Thomas and Caroline Gotch travelled a great deal and came and went from Newlyn until 1887 when they finally settled. She continued to paint until 1906 having been accepted regularly by the Royal Academy from 1890–95 and at the Paris Salon in 1897 and 1898 where she was awarded second and third medals. Very little work by Caroline Gotch survives today; there are some photographs in black and white, which show her composition was sophisticated and that she often painted children and women at home. We also know from old photographs that she painted typical Newlyn subjects such as *In midst of Life we are in Death* (1891) (whereabouts unknown) which is a scene set in a cottage where a family surrounds a dead man lying on a stretcher on the floor, probably drowned at sea.

Tom and Carrie Gotch made their first house in Newlyn, The Malt House, a centre of social activity. In 1888 they held a party for Frank Bramley after the success of his painting *A Hopeless Dawn* at the Royal Academy. Forbes described The Malt House as 'a charming house, under whose hospitable roof a genial host and hostess have done so much to promote and encourage that feeling of good fellowship which has always existed amongst us — the home of Mr and Mrs Gotch.' Forbes had described Tom and Caroline Gotch on first meeting with derision. He called Gotch 'a weak sort of creature' and compared him to an unmade bed in his appearance. Mrs Gotch he thought of as 'very aesthetic and untidy.' However he later warmed towards both of them possibly influenced by their involvement in the amateur theatricals — both had good voices and enjoyed singing.

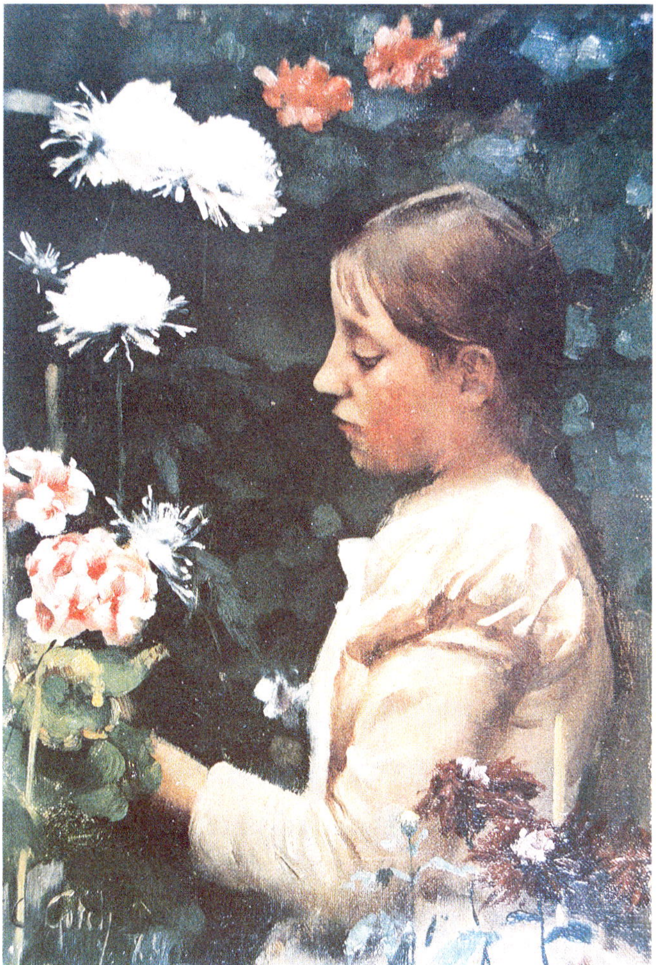

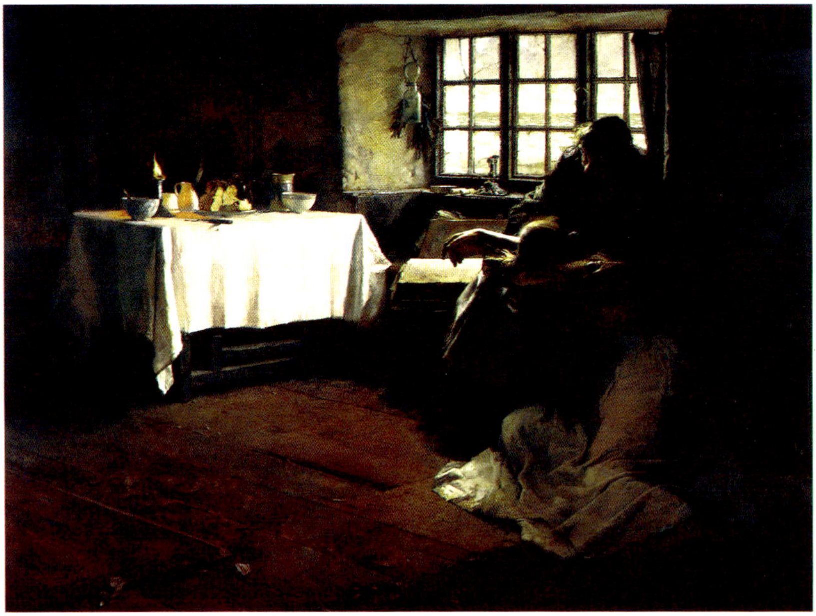

Frank Bramley (1857–1915)

Frank Bramley trained at Lincoln School of Art and Verlat's Academy in Antwerp. The dark tones of Northern European painting were a great influence on Bramley's style of painting. He exhibited works with a mainly Flemish subject at the Royal Birmingham Society of Artists from 1878. He then went to Venice in 1882 or 1883 with a friend William Logsdail. There was no school of art in Venice as such; there were not even official studios, just rooms with good light and access to models. Although it was an attractive place to paint, in the winter it was very cold and eventually the climate caused Bramley's health to fail and he had to leave. The picture he showed at the Royal Academy of Venice demonstrated his preoccupation with the figure rather than with scenery. The clothed figure placed in interiors continued to be his favoured subject in his Newlyn paintings. Bramley came to Newlyn in the winter of 1884, possibly persuaded there by his friends William Wainwright (1855–1931) and Edwin Harris. At 29 he was the same age as Stanhope Forbes who had also just arrived. The two artists were never to become friends but had mutual respect for each other's work. Bramley took lodgings in a top room of a small cottage on the corner of Belle Vue.

Much of Bramley's painting style up until about 1900 was firmly based on using the square brush technique that he had acquired in Antwerp. He used it particularly in his small studies. It was an ideal way of getting the basic tonal structure and composition of a painting down without the distraction of detail. His finest social realist painting was *A Hopeless Dawn* (1888) (Tate Gallery), which was bought by the Chantrey Bequest for the nation and was seen as a trademark Newlyn painting. The subject of human loss at sea was a frequent one portrayed by the Newlyn painters but this was probably regarded as the

30
Frank Bramley
A *Hopeless Dawn*, 1888
oil on canvas
123x167.5cm
(Tate Gallery)

31
Frank Bramley
A *Truce* 1912
oil on canvas
97.5x75cm
(Royal Cornwall Museum, Truro)

most successful one. Stanhope Forbes thought it a great painting. He wrote to his mother 'We saw Frank Bramley's picture which is not only good for him, but I think one of the finest pictures I ever saw. It will well establish his reputation I feel sure.'[19] When it was exhibited at the Royal Academy, Bramley had placed a quote from the art critic and writer Ruskin next to the painting which emphasized its religious overtones. 'Human effort and sorrow going on perpetually from age to age; waves rolling for ever, and faithful hearts wasting and sickening for ever, but brave lives dashed away about the rattling beach like weeds for ever; and still, at the helm of every lonely boat, through starless night and hopeless dawn, His hand, who spreads the fisher's net over the dust of the Sidonian palaces, and gave unto the fisher's hand the keys of the Kingdom of Heaven.' The religious ideas behind the painting are further emphasized in the work itself with a print of Raphael's cartoon 'Christ giving the keys to St Peter', on the right hand wall and an open book, probably the family Bible, on the window seat. The dim light of dawn and a single candle create a perfect opportunity for Bramley to show his skill at painting subtle tonal ranges. In fact the painting is almost monochrome which emphasizes the sombreness and the gravity of the subject. The candle in the window was seen as a symbol of the faith of the loving wife and family.

Women in domestic interiors were also the main subject of other Bramley paintings, such as *Primrose Day* (1885) (Tate Gallery) and *Domino* (1886) (Crawford Art Gallery, Cork). These are very calm, quiet paintings of female figures seated at tables. The tonal subtlety of these paintings, particularly *Domino* is shown by his brilliant use of white, a colour notoriously difficult to use in painting. Bramley seemed to deliberately set up scenarios, which forced him to paint the subtle hue changes caused by shadow. *Domino* was exhibited at the Royal Academy in 1886 and was hung 'on the line' and even though not picked out by the critics it was the 'first substantial interior scene in oils by a Newlyn artist and was probably a significant influence.'[20] *Primrose Day* was also a socio-political statement. The clue is in the print on the wall, which is a portrait of Benjamin Disraeli, England's Prime Minister from 1874–1880. The anniversary of his death was marked for many years and was known as Primrose Day and the preservation of his memory became a political act as the Liberals took office, the Primrose League being set up to promote Disraeli's conservative ideals. One of its aims was to promote the integration of people from different socio-economic backgrounds and particularly supported the role of women in society. Hence the use of a young girl as a model in Bramley's painting.

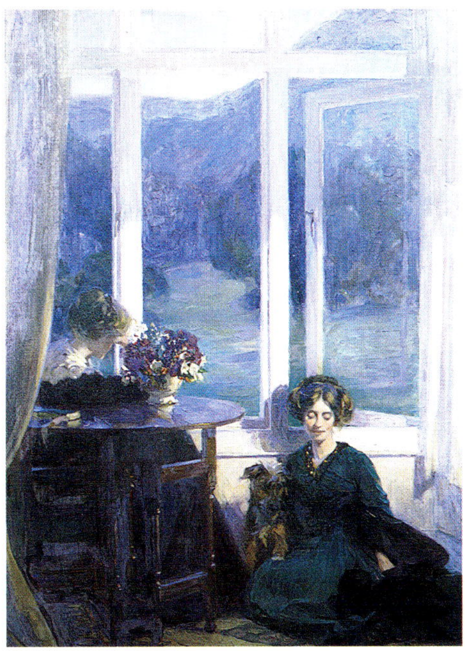

In 1895, Frank Bramley finally left for Droitwich in the Midlands and settled in Grasmere in Westmorland near his wife Katherine Graham's family home. His later work, of which *A Truce* (1912) (Royal Cornwall Museum) — referring to the truce between the cat and the dog — is typical, was sentimental and anecdotal reflecting the conventions of the time. Bramley died at 58 in London after suffering from a crippling illness.

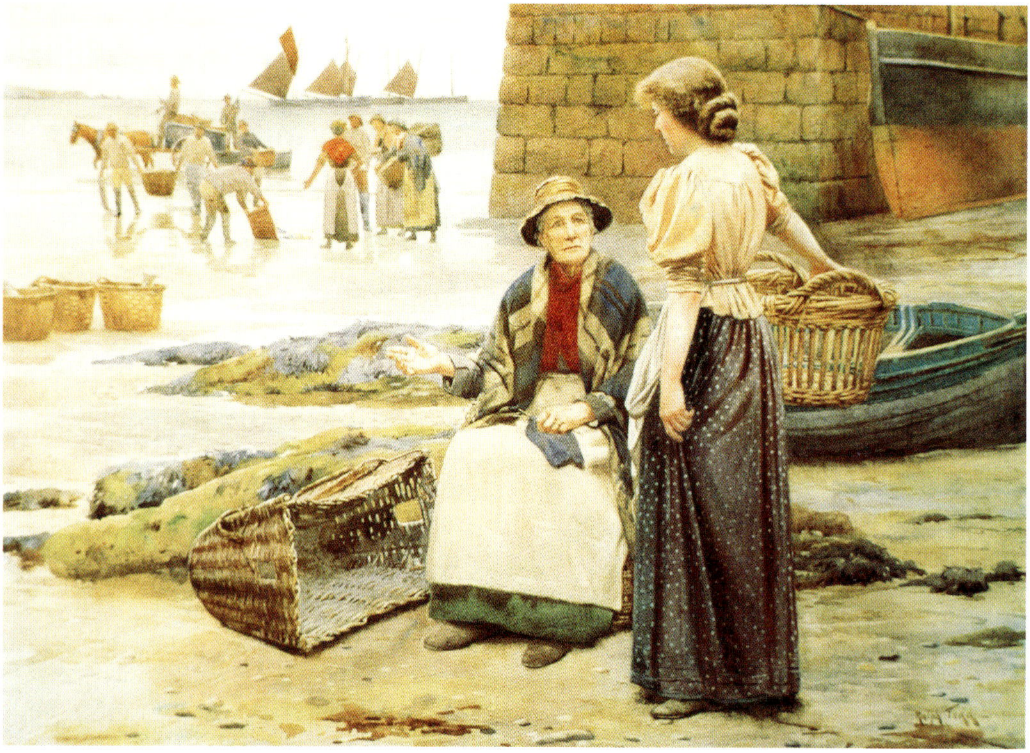

Ralph Todd (1856–1932)

As with all schools of art there are some artists who have more skill and talent than others and there are some who gain far greater publicity. But those who are not regarded as the 'greats' are equally important in telling the story of the Newlyn School. Ralph Todd is regarded by most art historians as falling into the latter category. He exhibited at the Royal Academy only three times, in 1885, 1887 and 1893. However, his skill at watercolour was considerable and although lacking the dynamism of Langley's work, his paintings had an aesthetic quality of their own. His colours were very soft and his compositions of figures, usually women, sitting on the beach or the quay were very still, giving an overall effect of peace and serenity.

Todd came to Newlyn in 1883 after training at the South Kensington School where he had won several prizes and had studied in Paris, the Netherlands and Belgium. He met Stanhope Forbes in Quimperlé, France in 1882 and they became great friends in Newlyn. But Forbes did not recognise Todd as an artist with any talent and thought 'He has no art in him and were he to paint forever would do no good work.'[21] Todd suffered from a lack of financial support as he was cut off when his wealthy father remarried. Despite Todd's financial constraints he worked hard at his painting. There are many drawings and sketchbooks in both Penlee House and The Royal Cornwall Museum's collections. He drew

32
Ralph Todd
Harvesters of the Sea
date unknown
watercolour
(Royal Cornwall Museum, Truro)

33
Ralph Todd
Primrose Day 1885
oil on canvas
45.8x35.5 (Penlee House Gallery and Museum, on loan from Newlyn Art Gallery)

mainly boats, cottage interiors and people. A good example of Todd's love of painting the boats and fishwives on the quay in watercolour is *Harvesters of the Sea* (date unknown) (Royal Cornwall Museum).

Todd also made an oil painting on the same subject of primroses in the same year as Bramley — *Primrose Day* (1885) (Penlee). The compositions are very similar with a young girl sitting at a table to the right of the picture with a vase of primroses and some spring blossom on the table. Todd's picture is not such an overtly political statement as Bramley's as the print on the wall depicts children playing and the overall mood of Todd's painting is not so dark in its range of colours. Bramley's painting uses the square brush technique, and although Todd did apply this brushwork to some pictures, his use of line and a clearer focus to his painting is much more evident here.

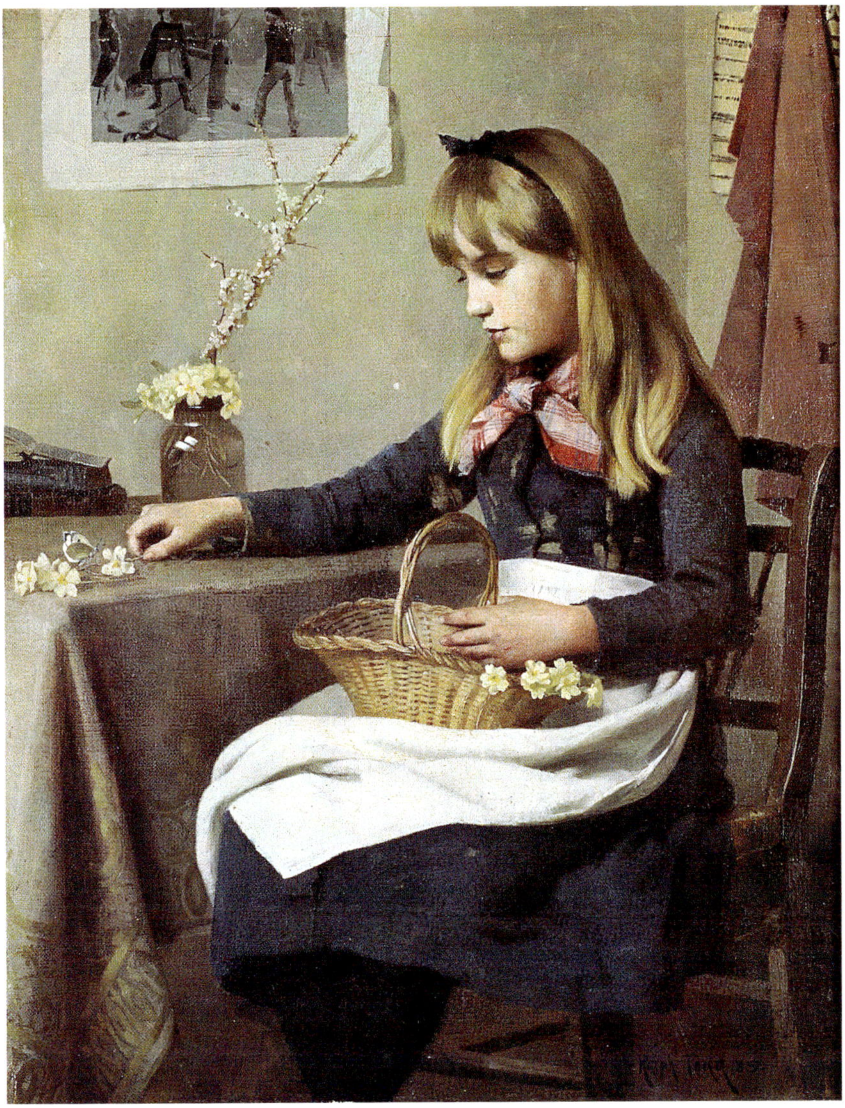

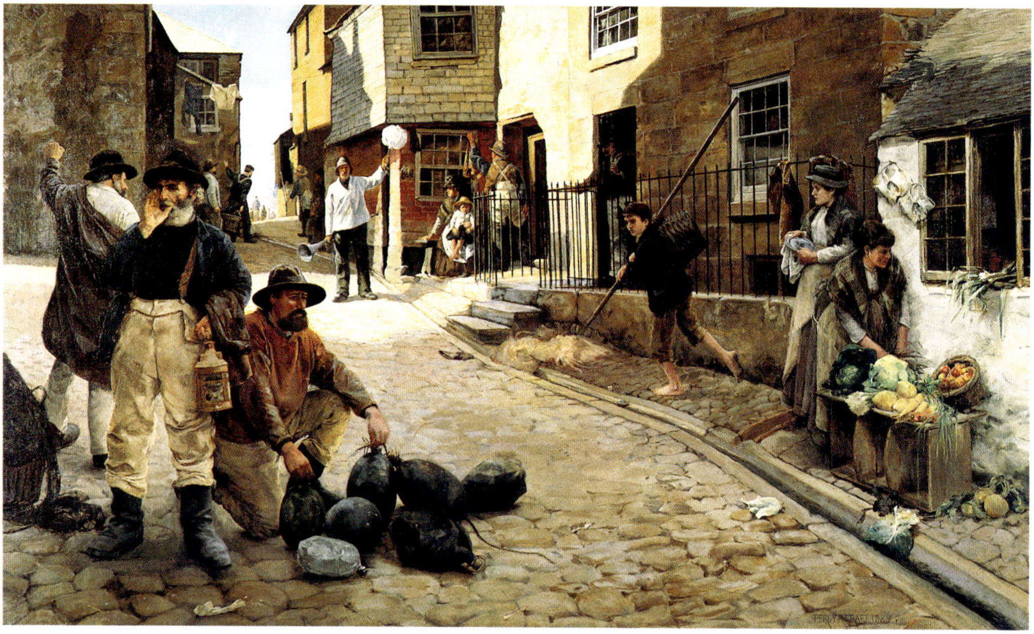

Percy Robert Craft (1856–1934)

Percy Craft was another Newlyn painter who focused much of his work on the fishing industry, although with a less mournful emphasis than Langley yet with just as much drama. Percy Craft had started out as an actor and some of his paintings have an element of theatrical composition. He came to Newlyn in 1885 with his wife Alice. By this time Newlyn had become a very successful fishing port, helped by the building of a 700ft long pier to shelter the harbour from the southerly gales and provide extra moorings for the growing fishing fleet and a lighthouse at the entrance. In 1886 the river was diverted so that a longer pier could be built which encircled the harbour. This work was completed in 1894 along with the harbour road, which connected the two parts of the village. The beach, which had been a subject for many of the painters, was covered with sheds where the fish were sold.

Catching or 'seining' shoals of pilchards from Land's End to Falmouth, Fowey and Mevagissey had become a major attraction for artists and visitors. Percy Craft made the depiction of pilchards being caught the subject of several of his most successful paintings. One called *Hevva! Hevva!* (1889) (Penlee) was painted in St Ives where he had moved in 1887. It is a street scene depicting the huer, the man whose job it was to spot the shoal of pilchards at sea. Fishing law dictated that no nets could be shot before the fishing boats were at least three miles offshore. His cry 'Hevva!' shouted through the metal trumpet was to alert the 'seiners', as they were known, that a shoal had been spotted. The seiners were the men who collectively owned the seine boats, nets and pilchard cellars ashore.

34
Percy Craft
Hevva! Hevva!
1889
oil on canvas
123x204.5cm
(Penlee House
Gallery and
Museum)

35
Percy Craft
Tucking a School of Pilchards (On the Cornish Coast) 1897
oil on canvas
143.5x212cm
(Penlee House
Gallery and
Museum)

In Percy Craft's other major work painted eight years later *Tucking a School of Pilchards (On the Cornish Coast)* (1897) (Penlee) the process of securing the shoal of pilchards by three seine boats is painted in great detail. Here the three boats are joined by many other vessels. Tucking the pilchards is when the shoal of fish has been brought in a net to shallow waters by the seine boats and the nets are emptied from the top, thus keeping the fish fresh in the water for a lot longer then if they had been caught out at sea. This painting was shown at the Royal Academy in 1897.

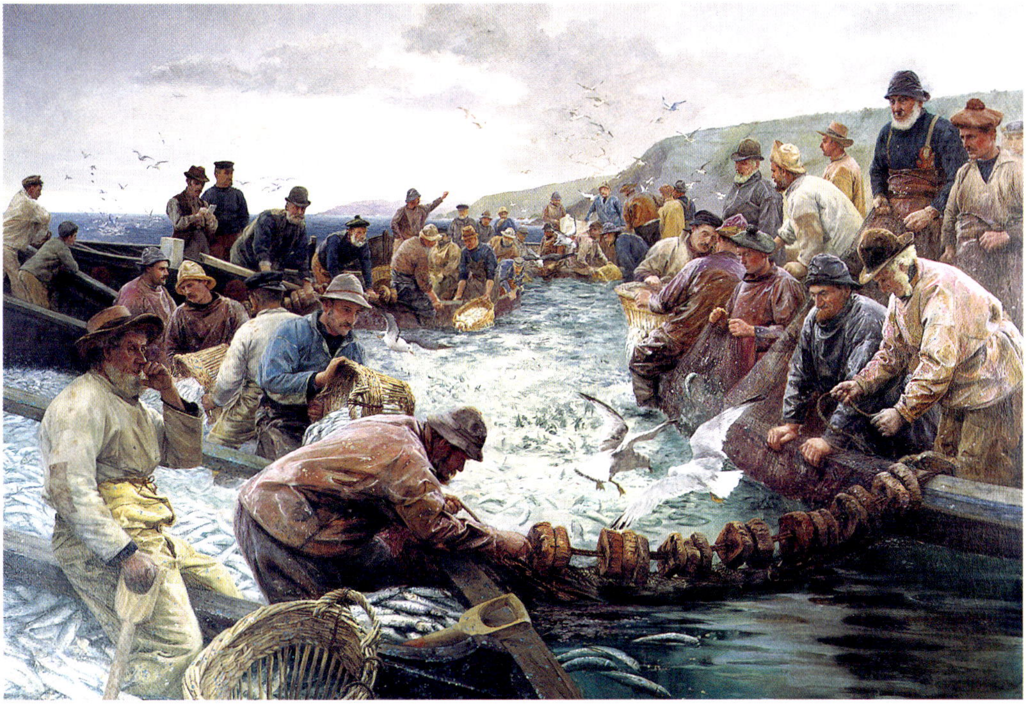

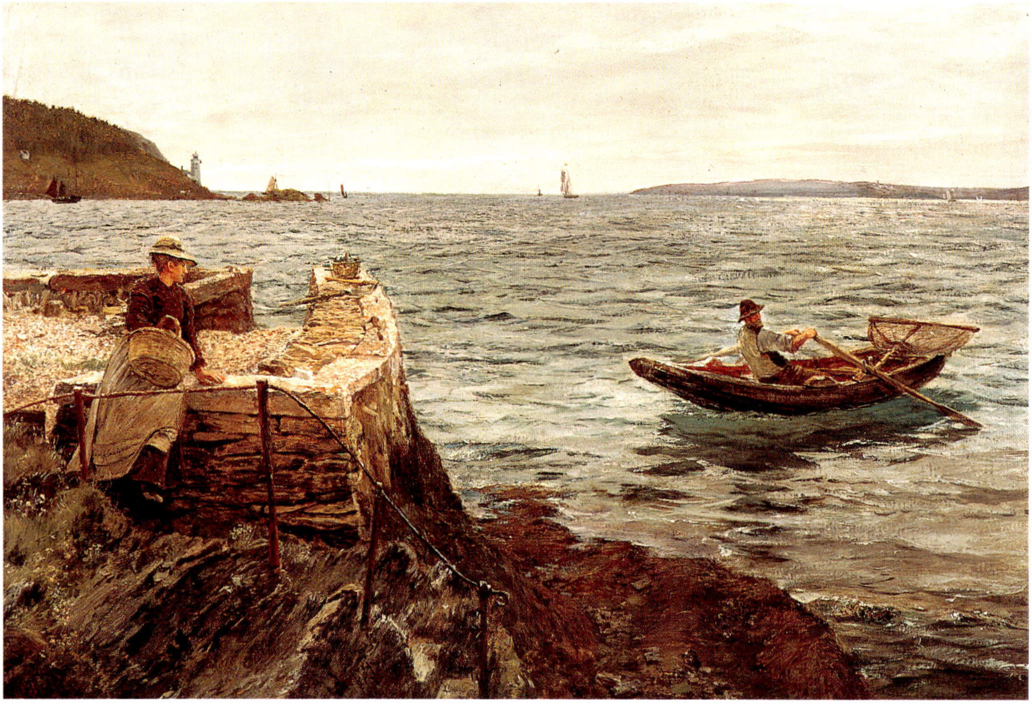

Charles Napier Hemy (1841–1917)

Charles Napier Hemy moved to Falmouth in 1881 in search of a new subject and made the town his home for the rest of his life. Hemy, like Henry Tuke after him, painted on boats which he converted into studios. His first was an old seine boat called the Vanderveld, this was replaced after it was shipwrecked, by the Vandermeer, a 19m yacht. Thus Hemy was close to the sea, which adds to the power of his maritime work. Hemy's painting *The Shrimper's Daughter* (1892) (Plymouth) is typical of his many coastal scenes dominated by the sea but showing local features such as St Anthony's lighthouse in the background and local fishermen in their boats in the foreground. Hemy was elected an associate of the Royal Academy in 1898 and became a full member in 1910.

Although Hemy lived in Falmouth he was a friend to many of the painters in Newlyn and like them painting the sea and fishing scenes. It was possibly unfortunate for Percy Craft that Charles Napier Hemy entered a very similar painting for the Royal Academy in 1897 entitled *Pilchards* (Tate Gallery) which was bought by the Chantrey Bequest. Hemy was an established artist by this time with a considerable reputation having exhibited at the Royal Academy since 1865. Hemy had been interested in pilchard fishing as a subject in 1885, when he painted a watercolour *How We Caught the Pilchards* (Walker Art Gallery, Liverpool). It is similar to Percy Craft's painting as it shows a close up of the men leaning over the boats surrounding the fish. Hemy's final oil painting of 1897 is less intense as he paints it further back from the action, but the visual dynamic of the painting is in the strong horizontal

36
Charles Napier Hemy
The Shrimper's Daughter 1892
oil on canvas
61x91.5cm
(Plymouth City Museum and Art Gallery)

37
Charles Napier Hemy
Falmouth Town
1910
watercolour, bodycolour and gouache 47x69cm
(Falmouth Art Gallery Collection)

38
Charles Napier Hemy
Haul Aft!
date unknown
gouache on paper 122x214cm
(Falmouth Art Gallery Collection)

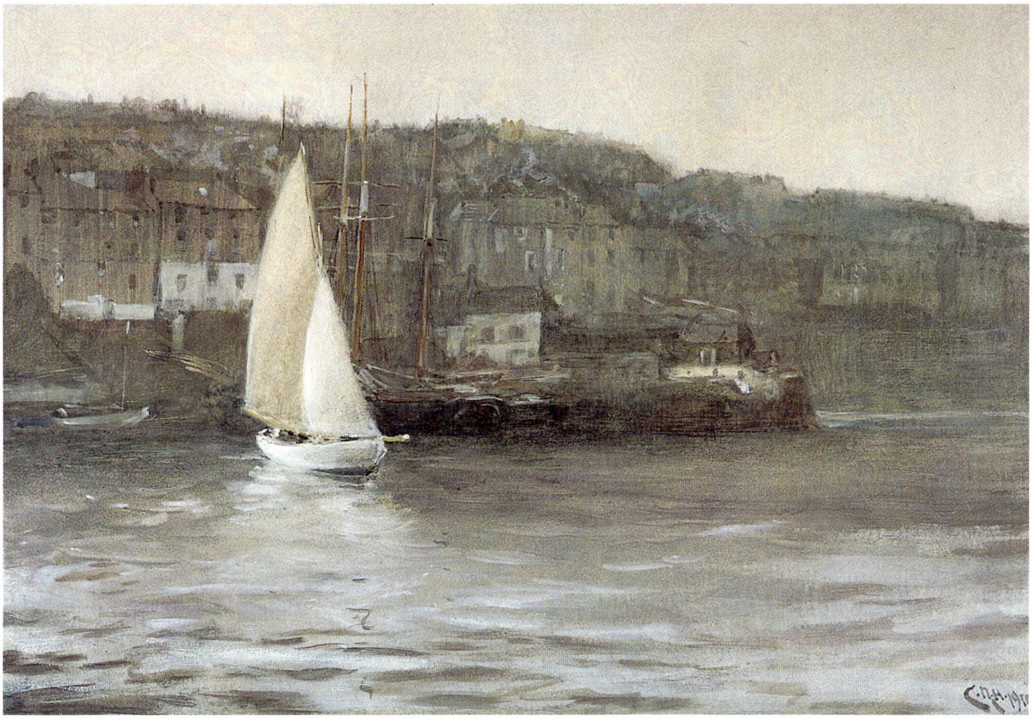

composition. This is bisected by the floats on the top of the nets, which act as two parallel lines that lead the viewer into the picture. The seine boats are depicted on either side of the nets creating the pincer movement that shows how the fishermen caught the pilchards.

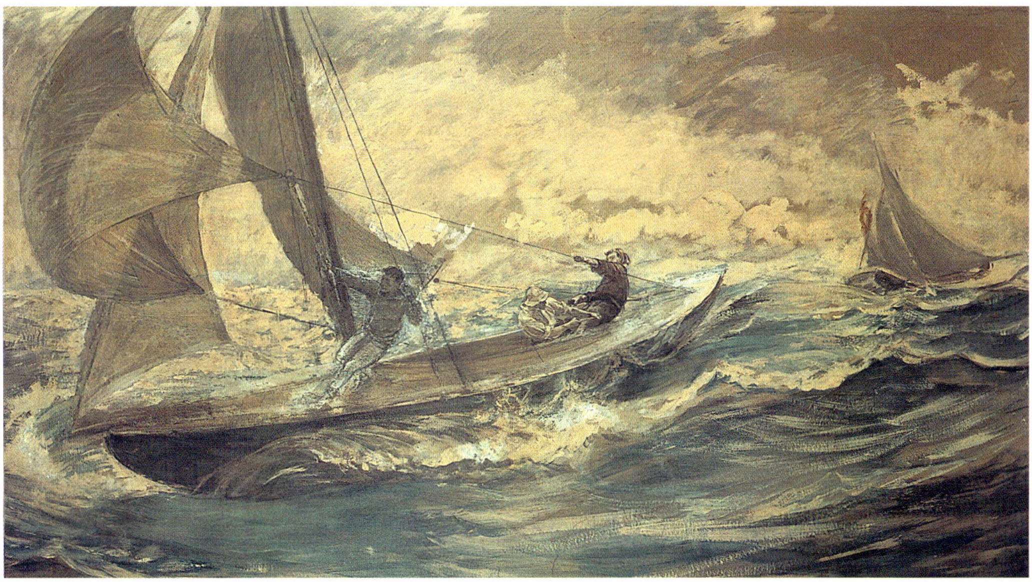

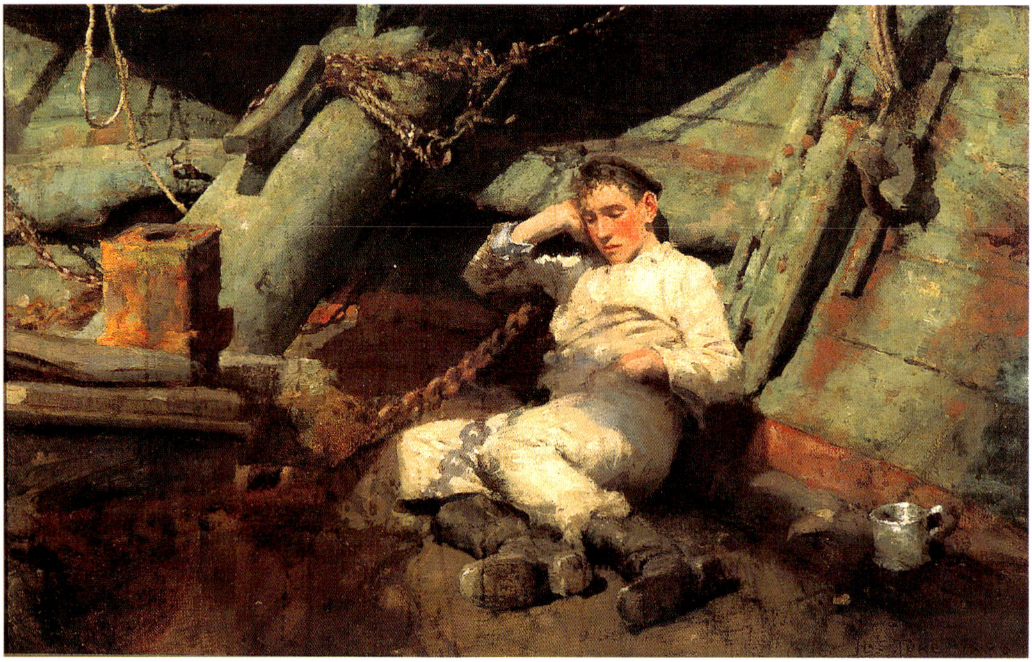

Henry Scott Tuke (1858–1929)

Henry Scott Tuke used portraiture as a way of having a steady income which subsidized his life of relative ease in Cornwall. He was a great friend of Thomas and Carrie Gotch and Chevallier Tayler and came to Newlyn in November 1883 living in the home of a local boat builder Philip Harvey. In the short time that Tuke spent in Newlyn, he made many sketches but few finished paintings. Apart from small portraits of Philip Harvey and his son Tom, he did two pictures in the tackle cellar, *Ship-Builders* (1883) (whereabouts unknown) and D*innertime* (1883) (whereabouts unknown). It was while based at Newlyn that he started to build on his work as a portrait painter with commissions from wealthy family friends such as Dr Falls in Bournemouth. At the same time he realised he could combine portrait painting with other subjects and began to place the figure in different settings, either outdoors on boats, by the beach, in the sea or in cottage or boat interiors. Tuke's first painting of boys in boats, which was to become his motif, was completed in Newlyn in 1884: called *Summertime* (whereabouts unknown) it depicts two local boys, John Wesley Kitching and John Rouffignac Cotton in Philip Harvey's punt Little Argo. Tuke found Newlyn inspirational and saw it after being away 'looking more bewitching than ever, I only wonder I didn't come here sooner, as it is now simply reeking with subjects.'

Whilst in Newlyn in the summers, 'Harry' Tuke seemed to spend most of his time sailing, fishing, swimming and socializing. In the summer of 1883, he sailed round to Falmouth on Ayerst Ingram's (1855–1913) (another maritime painter then based in St Ives, later to be based in Falmouth) boat and this trip made Tuke decide to return to Falmouth and have

39
Henry Scott Tuke
Taking a Spell 1886
oil on canvas
31.7x50.7cm
(Plymouth City Museum and Art Gallery)

40
Henry Scott Tuke
St Tropez 1907
watercolour
35.4x25.5cm
(Falmouth Art Gallery Collection)

41
Henry Scott Tuke
French Barque in Falmouth 1902
oil on canvas
50x60cm
(Falmouth Art Gallery Collection)

42
Henry Scott Tuke
Study of Boys Bathing 1912
oil on canvas
63.5x38.5cm
(Falmouth Art Gallery Collection)

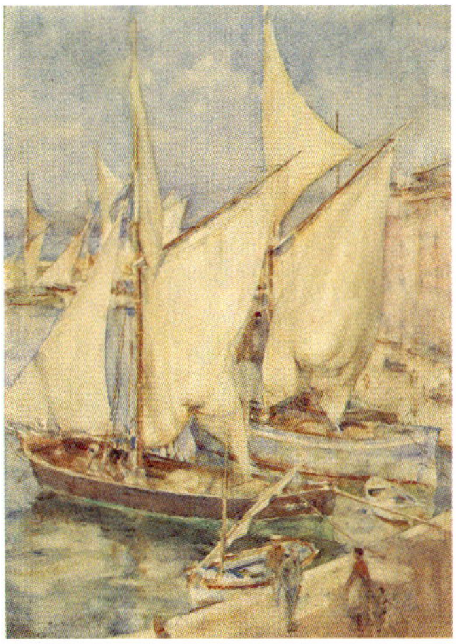

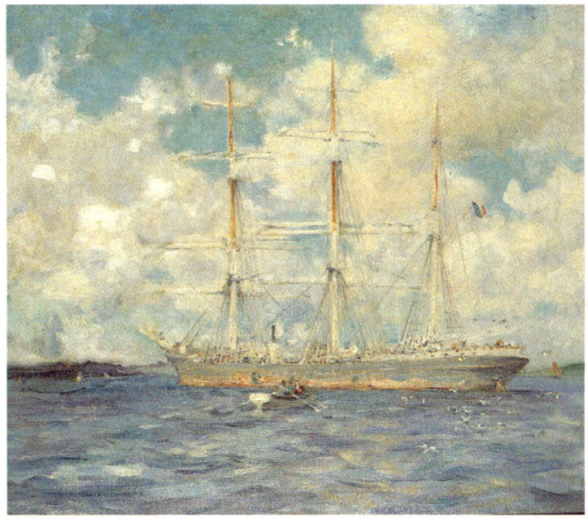

it as his base for the next 40 years. In 1885, Tuke finally moved into a cottage at Pennance Point, right by the sea. It was a secluded spot and he later built a large studio there. Mrs Fouracre, who remained Tuke's housekeeper for over 30 years, and her sons George and Richard, appeared as models in many of his paintings including *The Message* (1890) (Falmouth). This is a typical Newlyn interior painting of the time and sums up the country cottage idyll. Tuke used Pennance Cottage as the interior but made it appear to be a fisherman's cottage by adding items that refer to the fishing industry such as the nets hanging on the wall. It can also be seen in a series of portraits of Mrs Fouracre, the post boy William Martin, and the two Fouracre boys.

In June 1886 Tuke bought an old French brigantine called the Julie of Nantes which became his floating studio. Tuke undertook several major oils on the boat including *All Hands to the Pumps!* (1889) (National Maritime Museum, London), which was shown at the Royal Academy in 1889 and bought by the Chantrey Bequest. *Taking a Spell* (1886) (Plymouth) was probably also painted on the Julie. It is a different kind of portrait painting with the model, Jim Diamond, shown sleeping below deck. Tuke uses the mottled green of the wooden side of the boat and the brown of the rusting metal as a backdrop to the figure. Stanhope Forbes visited Tuke on the Julie in 1887 and wrote to his mother later 'Tuke showed us his pictures, which are simply beautiful. Gave us a wonderful tea under stranger circumstances than ever I took a meal before. It is a strange life to lead and only a man like Tuke could do it, but it suits him exactly, and he has subjects all around him such as he likes to paint best of all. We left him at last delighted with his

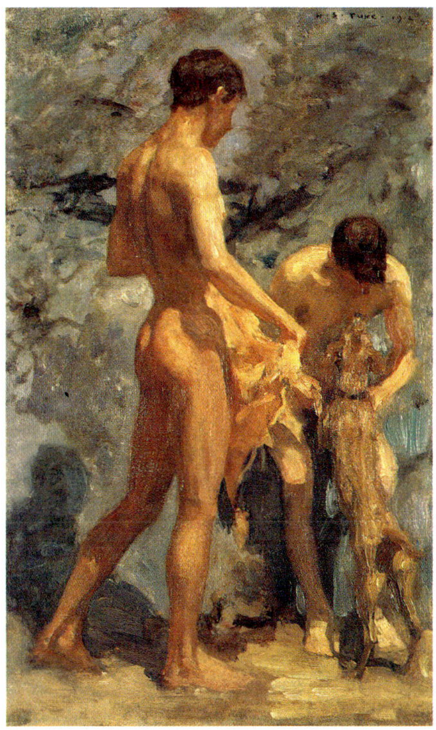

ship and his work.'[22] Tuke became famous for his figure compositions of both clothed and naked bathing boys on the beach. He was also an acclaimed maritime artist; there are many fine examples of his paintings of tall ships and other boats, in collections around the county, painted both in Cornwall and in the Mediterranean.

43
Henry Scott Tuke
The Message
1890
oil on canvas
60x50cm
(Falmouth Art Gallery Collection)

44
Elizabeth Forbes
School is Out
1889
oil on canvas
105.4x143cm
(Penlee House Gallery and Museum)

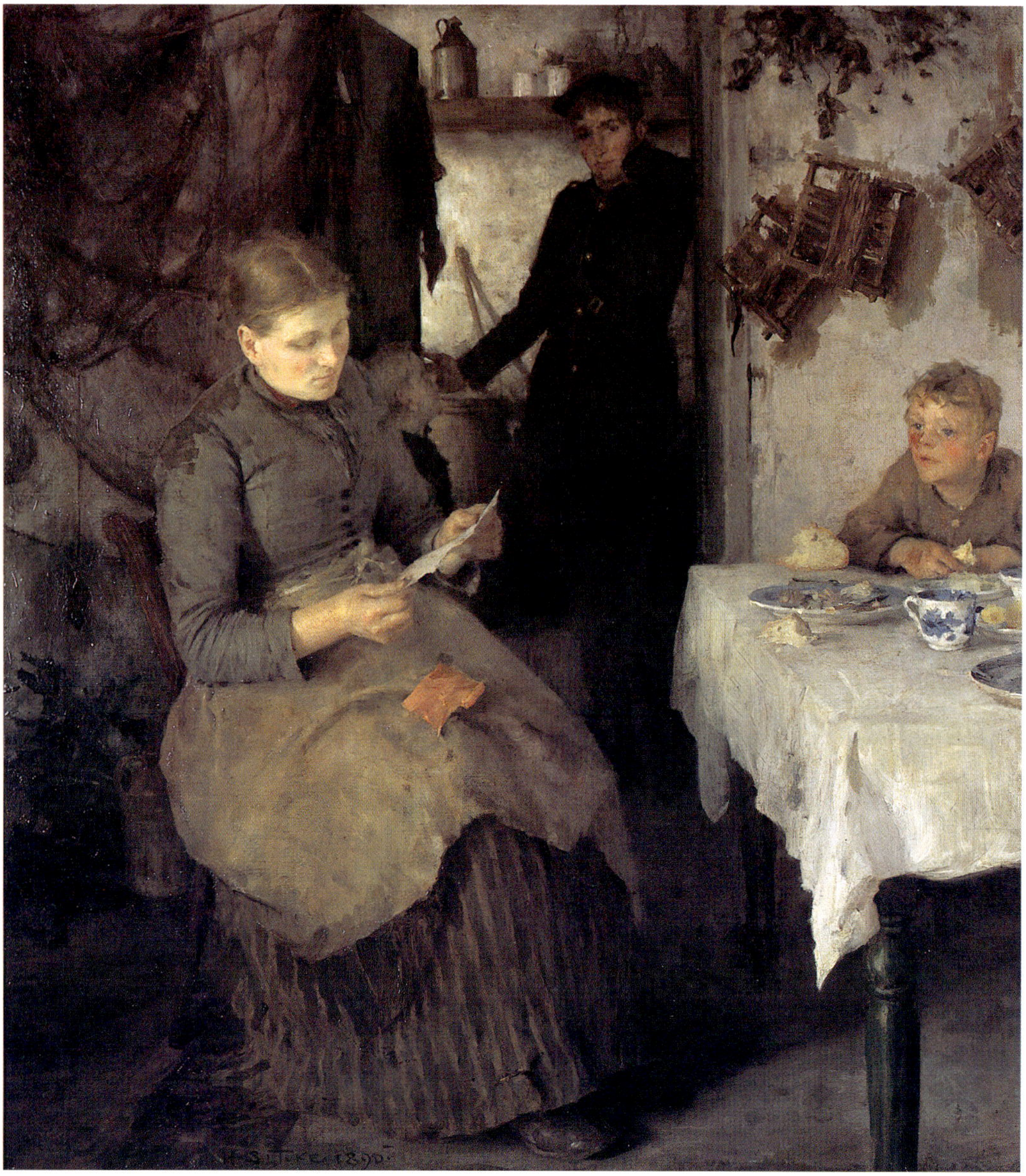

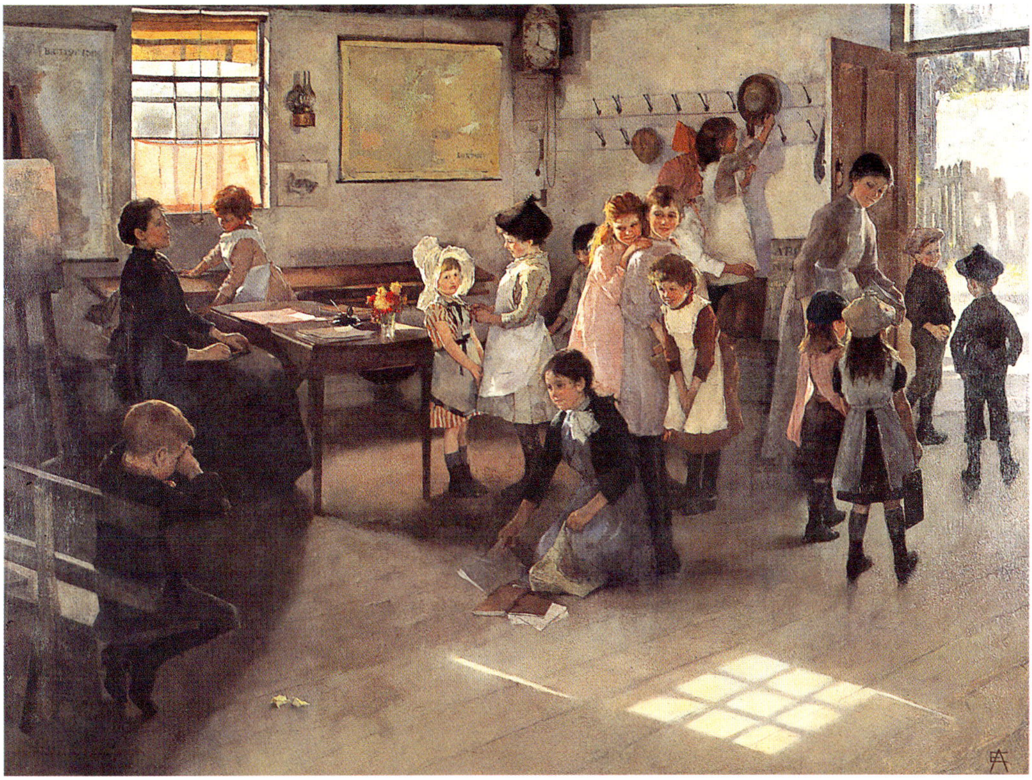

Elizabeth Adela Forbes (née Armstrong) (1859–1912)

Elizabeth Armstrong came to Newlyn in 1885 and took a studio in an old net loft and continued, even after her marriage to Stanhope Forbes in 1889, to depict the young as she had done in France. Her painting *Newlyn Maid* (date unknown) (Penlee) is probably an early work when Elizabeth Forbes was painting in the style of the Newlyn School before she developed her own particular visual language. It still shows her sensitivity to this young girl in the softness of her features and the subtlety in which she portrays her huge brown eyes. Forbes met Elizabeth Armstrong in November 1885 at the Harris' who had come to Newlyn in 1883. After his first encounter he wrote to his mother. 'She cannot be said to be pretty but a nice intelligent and ladylike girl.'[23] Soon he was in love with her and despite his mother trying to dissuade him, he asked her to marry him within six months.

Elizabeth Forbes' fascination with drawing children had begun in Pont Aven and developed in Newlyn. One very successful painting of an interior was of Paul village school where the children are just leaving. She called it *School is Out* (1889) (Penlee). This painting has a brightness and soft pink hue to the light, which suits the soft pink cheeks of the children she portrays. She places the children very naturally in the composition of the picture. The stars of this, and so many of her paintings over the coming years, were the children, showing her ability to convey their individual personalities.

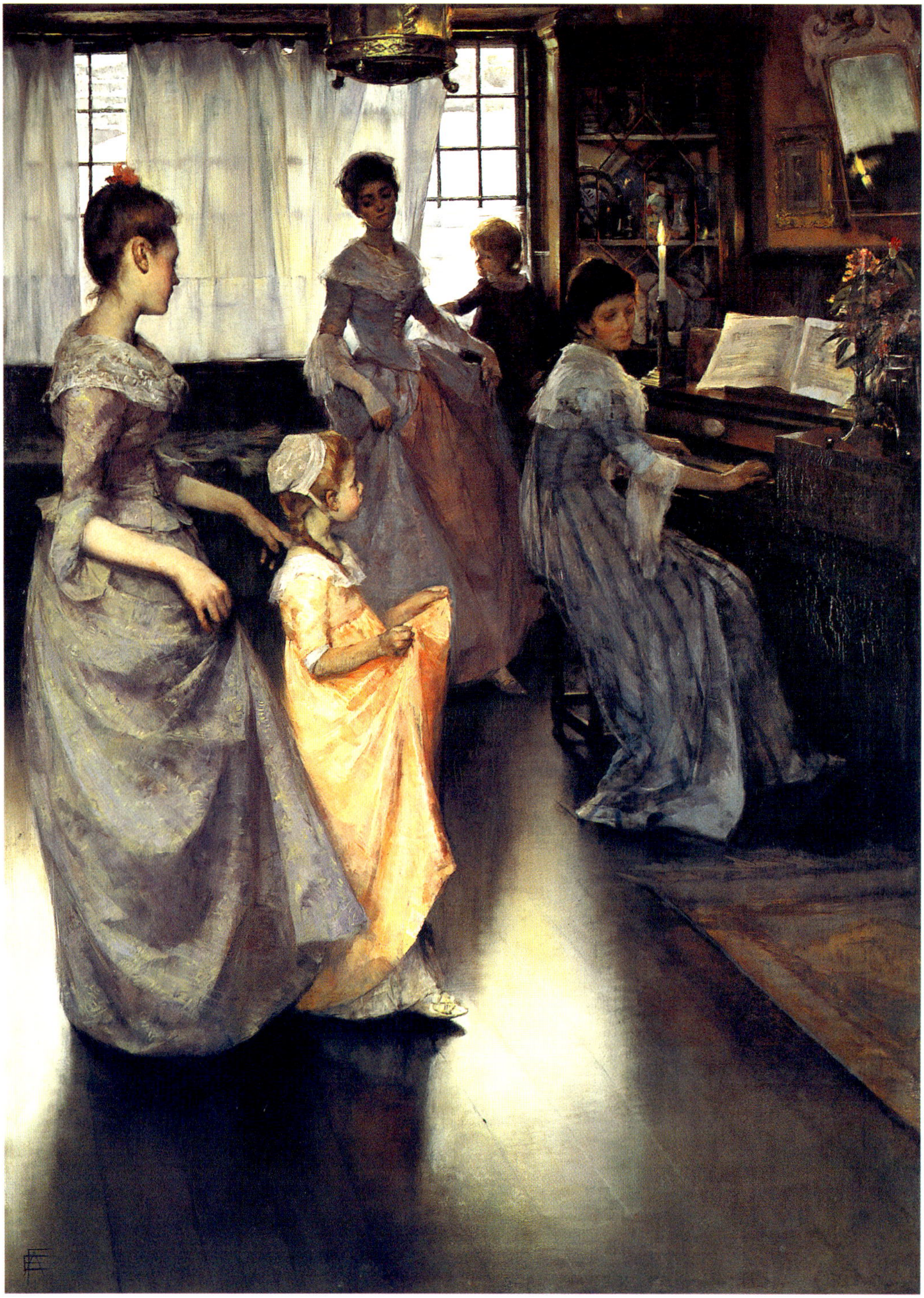

45
Elizabeth Forbes
A *Minuet* 1892
oil on canvas,
120 x 88.9 cm
(Penlee House Gallery and Museum, on loan from Private Collection)

46
Elizabeth Forbes
A *Newlyn Maid*
date unknown
oil on canvas
27.9x22.9cm
(Penlee House Gallery and Museum, on loan from Newlyn Art Gallery)

Elizabeth Forbes' dedication to *plein air* was important, but not always practically possible. She had a painting hut built for her that was moveable. In the 1890s she produced many gouache and charcoal studies of rural scenes in the countryside around Newlyn. They frequently included young lovers as models, or mothers with small children, reflecting her own joy at being a mother. Her son Alec was also a frequent model.

A *Minuet* (1892) (Penlee) is a study in light, the room is lit by a window at the back of the picture, but it is the reflected light on the polished wooden floor, which Elizabeth Forbes delights in. She uses a lighted candle on the piano as a focal point and creates another detail from its reflection in the mirror on the wall. It was this painting that caused one critic to note Elizabeth Forbes was 'one of the most accomplished of the Newlyn School, and at times, in colour and effects of light, surpasses her husband.'[24] At this time, Elizabeth Forbes, as well as Gotch and Rheam had become interested in mediaevalism. The inspiration came from Arthurian legend, fairy stories and Shakespeare. It referred back to the Pre-Raphaelite brotherhood and their interest in depicting such subjects. Elizabeth Forbes combined storytelling with a pursuit of *plein air* painting, dressing models in mediaeval costumes and placing them in the landscape. A *Dream Princess* (Royal Cornwall Museum) appeared in the Royal Academy summer show of 1897, alongside similar mediaeval-inspired works by Arthur Buckland, George Hitchcock, and E Blair Leighton, as well as fellow Newlyner, Thomas Gotch.

Elizabeth Forbes used Shakespeare as her inspiration for A *Woodland Scene: 'As You Like It'* (date unknown) (Royal Cornwall Museum); two girls look at a man who is carving a name in a tree dressed in period costume. It is a combination of gouache, charcoal and pastel on paper, which is quite a challenging combination of materials to use successfully, but she became very skilled at it. She had several exhibitions in London on the theme of children and childhood: at the Fine Art Society in 1900 'Children and Child Lore' and the Leicester Gallery's 'Model Children and Other People' in 1904. She won the praise of the critics for these exhibitions for her subtle insight into the beauty of childhood.

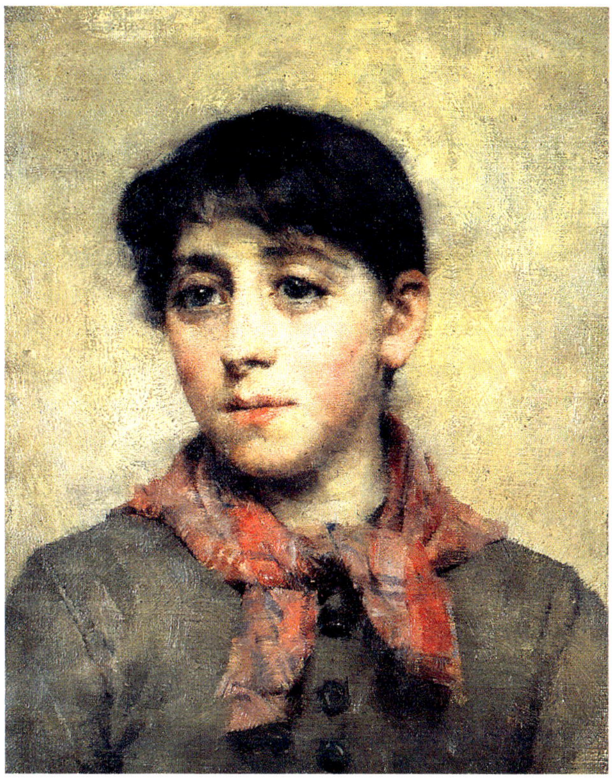

One of her greatest applications of imagination to her art was the unique illustrated book *King Arthur's Wood*, published in 1904. She had always loved fairy stories as she had often made up her own tales for her son. The

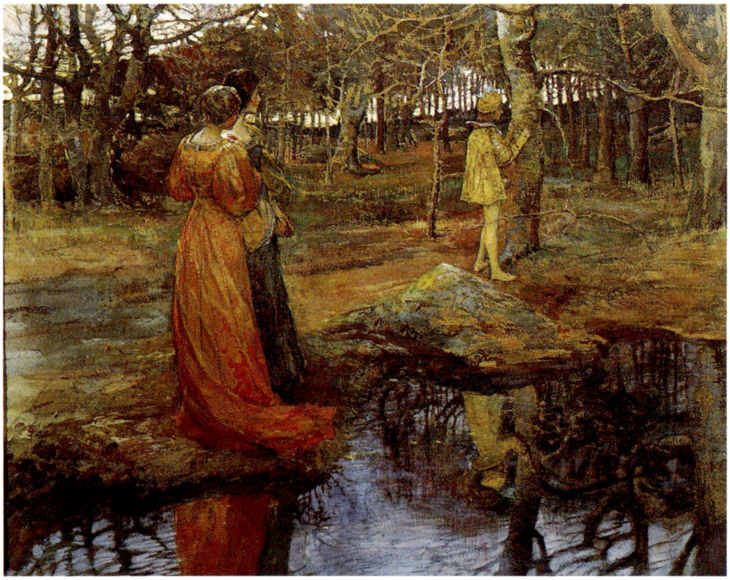

47
Elizabeth Forbes
A Woodland Scene: 'As You Like It'
date unknown
pastel
68x89cm
(Royal Cornwall Museum, Truro)

48
Elizabeth Forbes
At That Word
book illustration from 'King Arthur's Wood' 1899
published 1904
mixed media
30x42.5cm
(Private Collection)

illustrations, painted in 1899, are some of her finest watercolours and pastels. The hero of the story, a small boy, Myles, and a little girl, Noel, come to live in Cornwall with their Aunt Patience. The house stands close to the magic King Arthur's Wood. Myles finds a strange stone table in the middle of the wood and carelessly taps it. At once a little brown man appears and tells him that he is the keeper of Merlin's book. Myles then has a series of adventures and encounters. The book was dedicated to Elizabeth's son Alec who was about to leave for boarding school. Elizabeth also published a magazine called 'The Paper Chase' that included illustrations by her and other artists of the Newlyn School, as well as poems and short stories edited by Fryn Tennyson Jesse. It was intended to be a monthly magazine, but only two editions were produced, one in March 1908 and another in 1909. Her artistic career was cut short in 1912 by her death from cancer. She was 52.

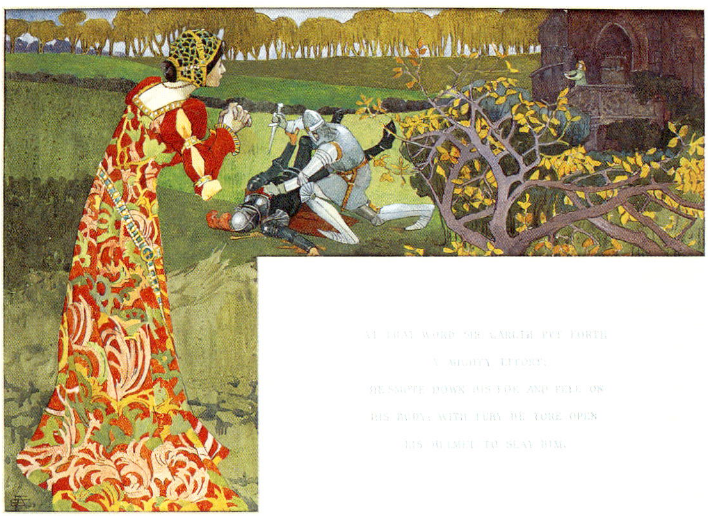

49
Fred Hall
In the Fields 1886
oil on canvas
80.5x38cm
(Penlee House Gallery and Museum)

50
Fred Hall
Josiah Wright
c1890
oil on canvas
(Royal Cornwall Museum, Truro)

Frederick Hall (1860–1948)

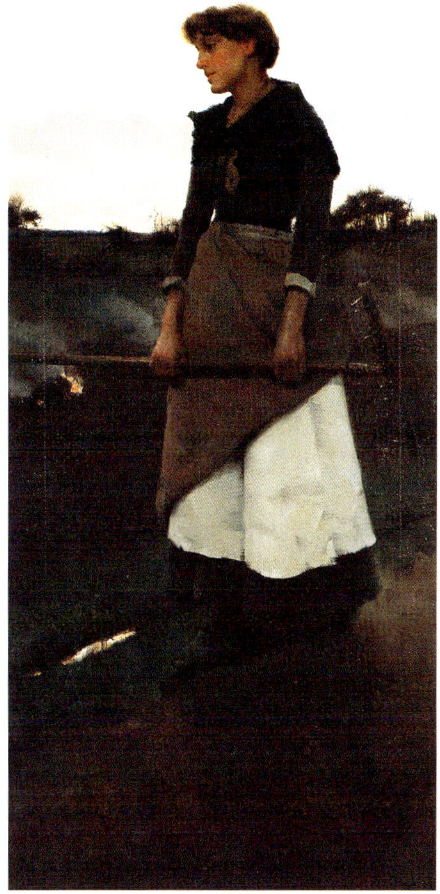

'Fred' Hall, as he liked to be known, was born in Yorkshire, attended Lincoln School of Art, Verlat's academy in Antwerp and first exhibited at the Royal Academy in 1883. He made a number of paintings in Newlyn, but by 1897 had moved away for good, finally settling in Newbury.

In the Fields (1886) (Penlee) is a powerful portrait of a young girl walking home from the fields carrying her work tool. She is silhouetted against an amazing sky signifying the end of a long day. This is a very dark painting and is a subtle study in tone observed in the fading light at dusk. This same young girl is also featured in a larger work of the same year: *Home From the Fields* (Private Collection).

In the painting of the farmer *Josiah Wright* (c1890) (Royal Cornwall Museum), the light comes from the right hand side this time and picks up the contours of the old man's face

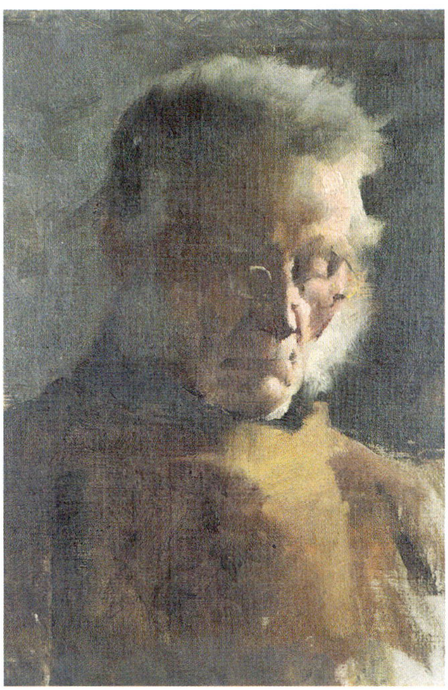

illuminating his white whiskers and his hard-bitten mouth. Hall uses the square brush technique to describe the overall shape of the head, but there is a softness to the painting in the glint of light bouncing off his gold rimmed spectacles and the orange and brown ochres used for the old man's tunic. Fred Hall was a confident portrait painter; more often the subject would be turned into a cartoon rather than taken seriously. He was described in the 'Cornishman' newspaper as 'something of a mystery'. It went on to say 'he looks painfully serious yet is a delightful, humorous caricaturist'.[25]

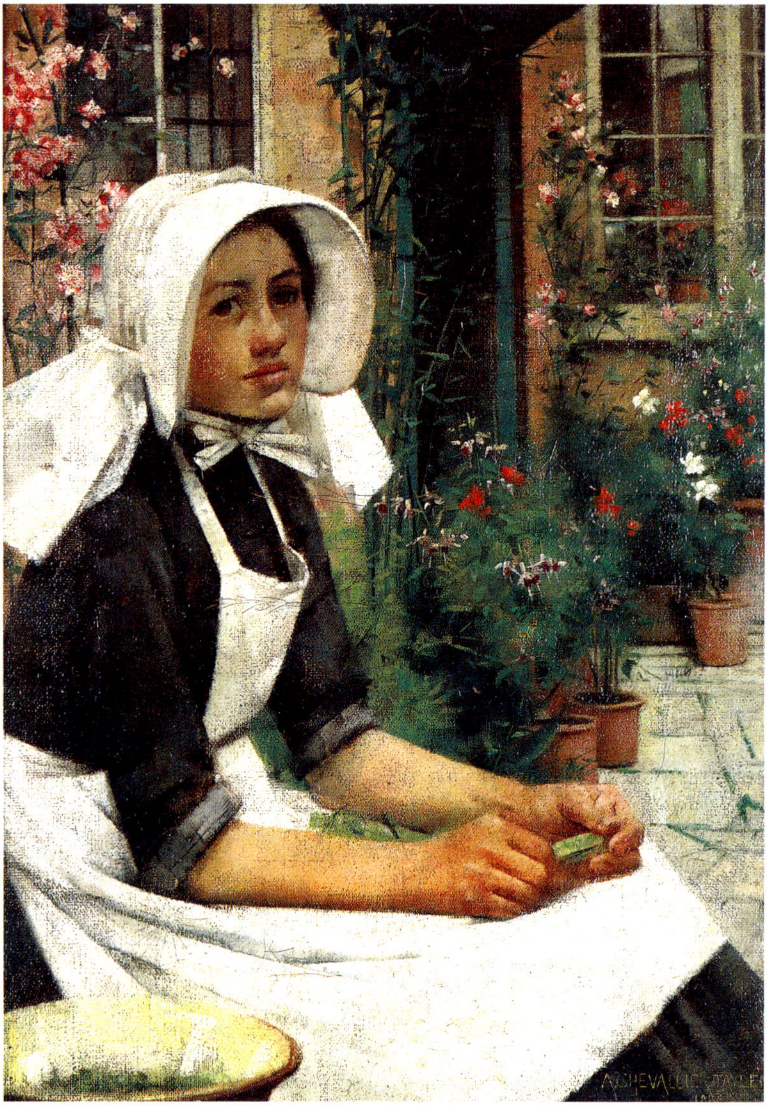

Albert Chevallier Tayler (1862–1925)

Shelling Peas (date unknown) (Penlee) is an example of a rural domestic scene by Albert Chevallier Tayler, who painted in Newlyn between 1884 and 1895. Born in Essex he went to the Slade to study after gaining a rare scholarship and then went on to Laurens' atelier in Paris for two years. Here he met Thomas Gotch and Jacomb Hood who became great friends, as well as Henry Scott Tuke. Tayler came to Newlyn in 1884 and stayed at Bellevue with Forbes. Tayler was also a painter of the fishing fleet with remarkable pictures such as *The Departure of the Fishing Fleet, Boulogne* of 1891 (City of Birmingham Museum and Art

51
Albert Chevallier Tayler
Girl Shelling Peas
date unknown
oil on canvas
38x28cm
(Penlee House Gallery and Museum)

52
William Teulon Blandford Fletcher
Bosham Harbour at Low Tide 1901
oil on canvas
50x78cm
(Penlee House Gallery and Museum)

Gallery). Tayler was however never particularly successful at selling his work and his subjects whilst in Newlyn reflected his strong Roman Catholic faith. By the turn of the century Chevallier Tayler's work had become sentimental and depicted middle class Edwardian dinner parties in opulent drawing rooms.

Shelling Peas is a particularly successful composition, with the bent arms of the girl echoing the corner of the canvas, which leads the eye of the viewer into the space of the picture. The traditional peaked cap she wears creates a tunnel shape casting a shadow over her face, which again is echoed in the shadowy doorway behind. There is a very sensitive use of colour in this painting with soft pinks and reds in the geraniums and fuschia.

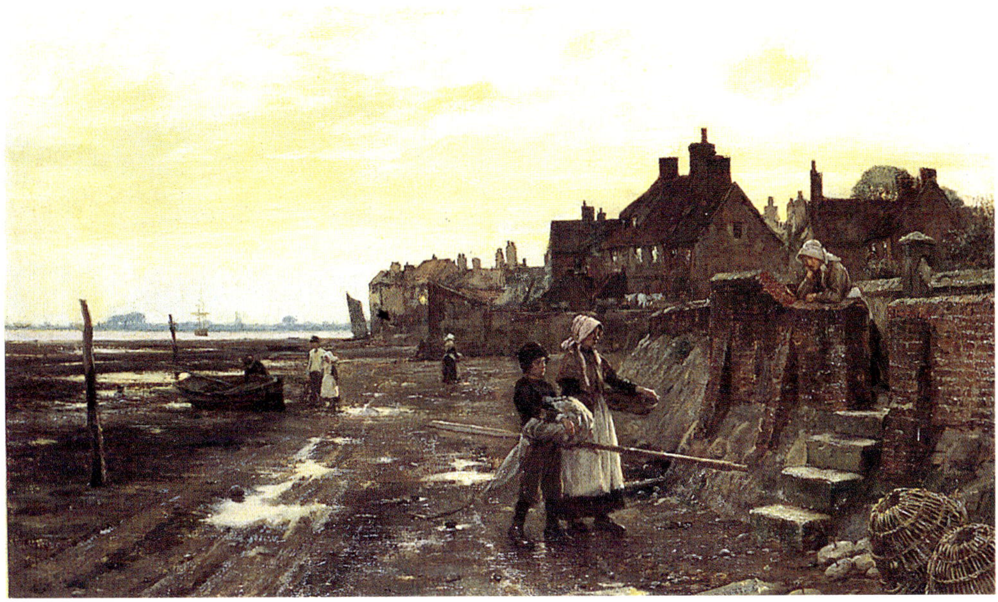

William Teulon Blandford Fletcher (1858–1936)

Despite his strong involvement with the colony, very little of William Teulon Blandford Fletcher's Newlyn work survives. He was known as a painter of village life all over Britain and abroad. He and his young wife Norah travelled the countryside together after they were married in 1894. Their journeys took them to Devon, Norfolk, Yorkshire, Kent, Sussex and Dorset. In total he is said to have visited every cathedral city and over 200 towns in Britain. He finally settled in Wescott, Dorking in 1904 and then in 1915 Northcourt, near Abingdon in Oxfordshire. There are only two examples of his work in Cornish collections: *Bosham Harbour at Low Tide* (1901) (Penlee) and *Beer, Devon* (1912) (Plymouth). Both these works show overcast skies and closely toned colours indicative of the Newlyn style. This was hardly surprising as Blandford Fletcher had trained with them and was a follower of Bastien-Lepage.

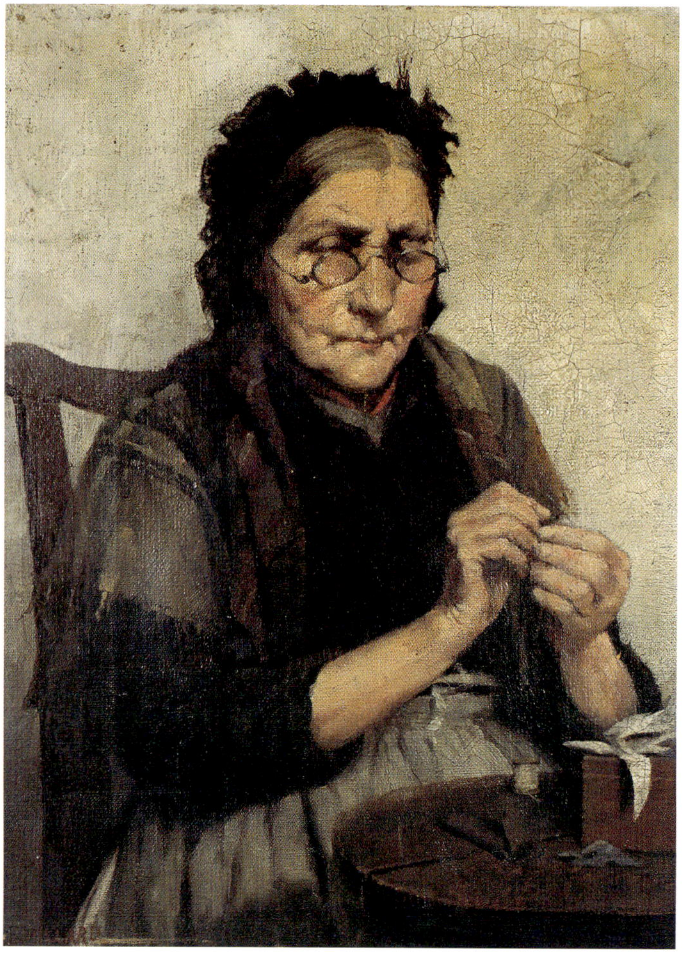

53
Fred Millard
The Thread of Life Runs Smooth as Yet c1895
oil on canvas
31.5x24.5cm
(Penlee House Gallery and Museum)

54
Fred Millard
Cornish Girl with a Basket of Primroses
date unknown
oil on canvas
55.5x39.5
(Royal Cornwall Museum, Truro)

Frederick Millard (1857–1937)

'Fred' Millard's painting of an old Newlyn fisherwoman *The Thread of Life Runs Smooth as Yet* (c1895) (Penlee) shows the concentration on the old woman's face as she tries to thread a needle. His painting *Cornish Girl with a Basket of Primroses* (date unknown) (Royal Cornwall Museum) is delightful portrait of a young maid. The rich yellows in her straw hat, shawl and basket contrast beautifully with her blue skirt and shirt. The painting could be associated with the paintings by Bramley and Ralph Todd of girls in interiors with primroses, which had a socio/political meaning.

Little is known of Fred Millard who came from Reigate in Surrey, other than he had a studio in Newlyn with Ralph Todd. Forbes documents his arrival in April 1884 and describes him as 'a decent fellow and an acquisition to our society.' Millard studied at Laurens' atelier when Tuke and Gotch were there between 1881 and 1882 as he appears in a photograph with them taken at the time. He exhibited at the Royal Academy in 1885, 1887, and 1888.

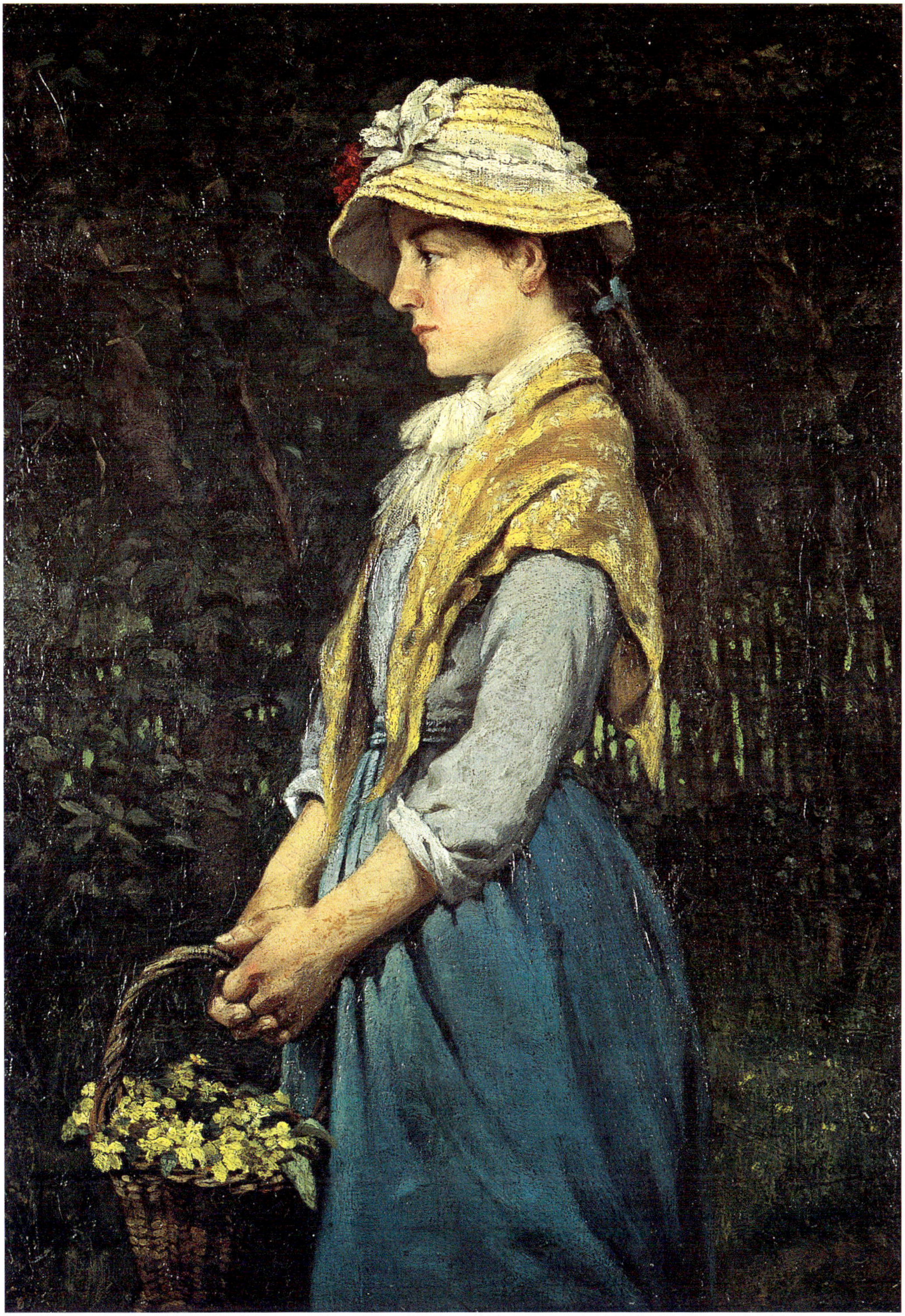

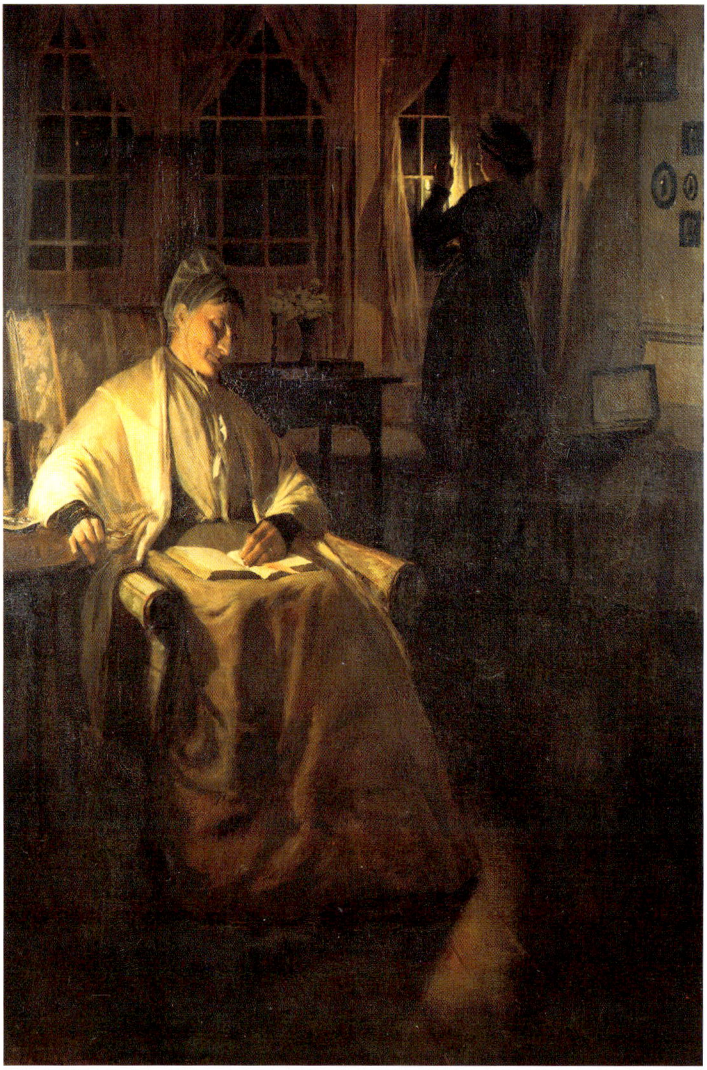

Norman Garstin (1847–1926)

A latecomer, Norman Garstin had travelled a great deal before settling in Newlyn in 1887. Some of the places he visited are represented by works such as *Saints House, Tangier* (1885) (Plymouth City Museum and Art Gallery), and A *Ravine Spain* (1886) (Plymouth City Museum and Art Gallery). These are small works painted quite loosely in oil on panel. Garstin had a natural technique, which leaned more to an impressionist style, probably gained from his time in Paris from 1880–1882. Garstin's panels were done very quickly. He preferred 'haze to brilliant sun. His is an art of suggestion by tonal variation rather than description. The miracle is that they convey so much information in so small a space.'[26]

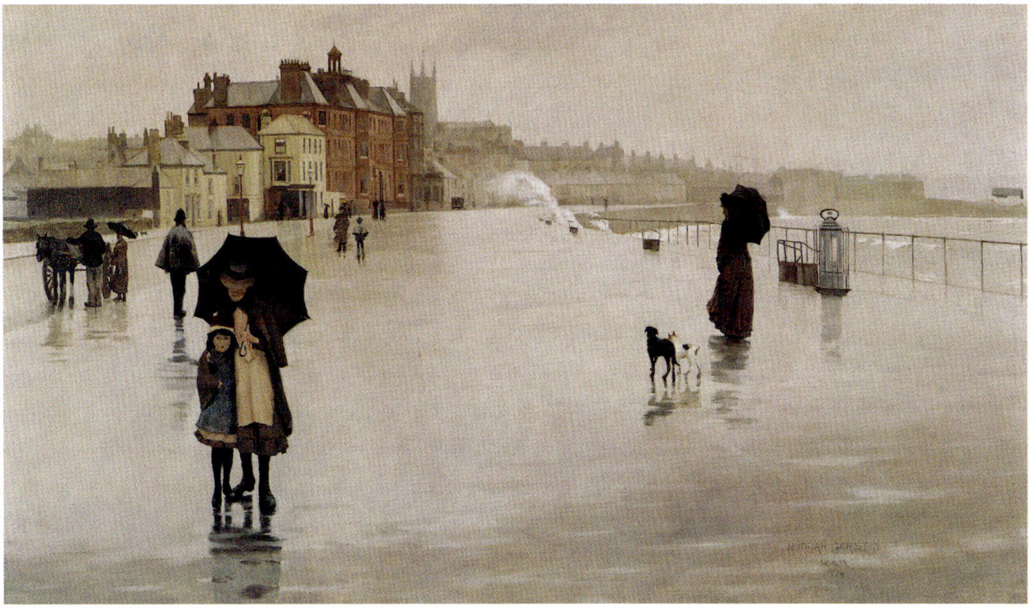

55
Norman Garstin
Her Signal 1892
oil on canvas
155.5x110.5cm
(Royal Cornwall
Museum, Truro)

56
Norman Garstin
*The Rain it Raineth
Everyday* 1889
oil on canvas
95x162.4cm
(Penlee House
Gallery and
Museum)

In 1890, Garstin and his wife with their two sons Crosbie and Denis moved to Penzance. He depicted local views with great accuracy with a reference to Japanese art in his composition. One of his most well known pictures is a view of Penzance from the promenade in the rain. *The Rain it Raineth Everyday* (1886) (Penlee). The Japanese reference can be seen in the asymmetry of this painting. It is a very static painting except for the white flash of a wave breaking over the sea wall of the promenade in the background. The painting was seen as very successful by his fellow Newlyn painters, but sadly was left out of the hang after being accepted by the Royal Academy in 1889. The title has been interpreted as Garstin taking a humorous look at his own circumstances. Although his talent was considerable he had great trouble in selling his work. He lost his inherited income which he had enjoyed whilst travelling and studying, because of mismanagement by the trustees of the estate; Garstin was declared bankrupt. He was able to supplement his income by writing on art, giving lectures and taking on art students both locally and abroad.

Norman Garstin's painting *Her Signal* (1892) (Royal Cornwall Museum) is a typical Newlyn portrait of an old woman but not typical of Garstin's work in general. This is a very dark painting and grim subject where as on the whole Garstin's paintings were a lot lighter and not so heavy in subject. When it was exhibited at the Whitechapel Gallery in 1902 an additional caption was placed next to the work saying 'the older woman, the sands of whose life are almost run out, has fallen asleep, while the girl has seized the moment to show the signal to the young, perhaps forbidden, love outside'.

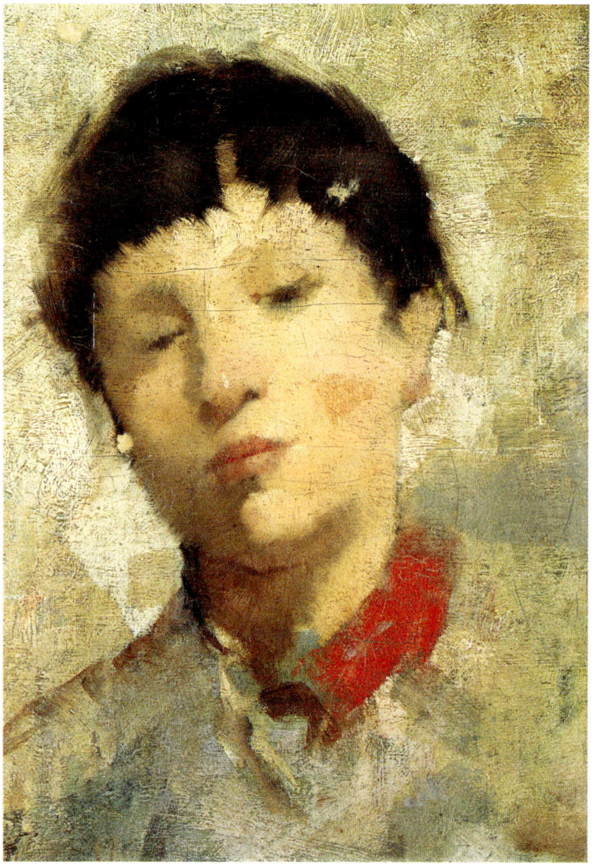

Leghe Suthers (1855–1924)

An early visitor to Newlyn in 1883, Suthers undertook several portraits using the square brush technique, for example *Anne Rowney of Newlyn* (date unknown) (Royal Cornwall Museum). Anne was painted by Suthers on more than one occasion. In this portrait she is caught looking down with one eye almost shut. The brushwork is very bold and creates a broken impressionistic surface.

Suthers studied at Verlat's Academy in Antwerp and was great friends with Fred Hall and Frank Bramley who also studied there. Later, he met Stanhope Forbes in Brittany. He went to paint in Venice and Venetian subjects dominated his early work shown at the Royal Academy. When in Newlyn, Suthers showed his work at Ralph Todd and Fred Millard's studio in October 1886. Never well known, Suthers is seen as one of the original Newlyn artists. His use of the square brush technique was probably why he was so closely associated with the School even though he was often away from the village and did not spend much time there.

56
Leghe Suthers
Anne Rowney of Newlyn
date unknown
oil on canvas
32x22.5cm
(Royal Cornwall Museum, Truro)

57
Henry Meynell Rheam
Gathering Daffodils
1907
watercolour
84x61cm
(Royal Cornwall Museum, Truro)

Henry Meynell Rheam (1859–1920)

The theme of costumed figures in the landscape was the dominant subject in Henry Rheam's work. He studied art in Germany as well as at Heatherly's in London and at Julian's academy in Paris. He came to Polperro initially and then was lured to Newlyn to bolster the Newlyn artists' cricket team. Rheam mainly worked in watercolour and although he undertook typical Newlyn scenes such as *Girl in Blue* (1891) (also known as *The Blue Lady*) he seems to have turned to more fanciful subjects in the 1890s. The Royal Cornwall Museum has four fine examples of this work including *The Dragon's Cave*, *Pandora's Box*, *The Mannequin* and *Gathering Daffodils* (1907). Rheam married Lucie Elliot in 1890 and lived in Penzance at White Lodge until he died in 1920.

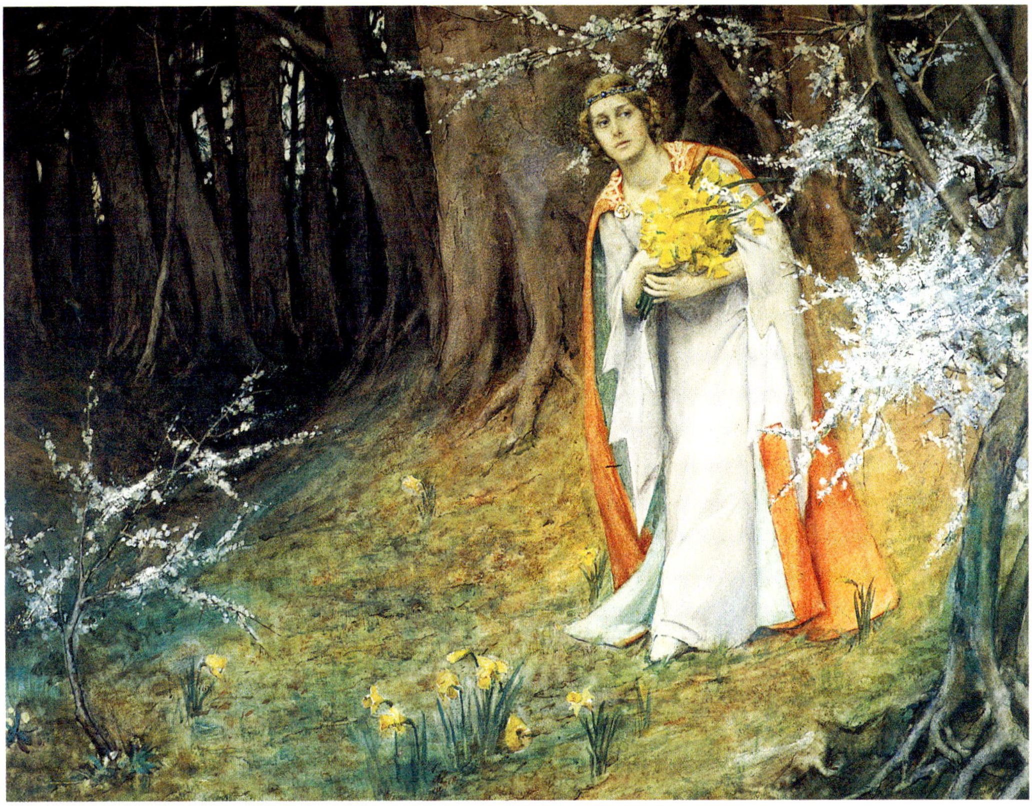

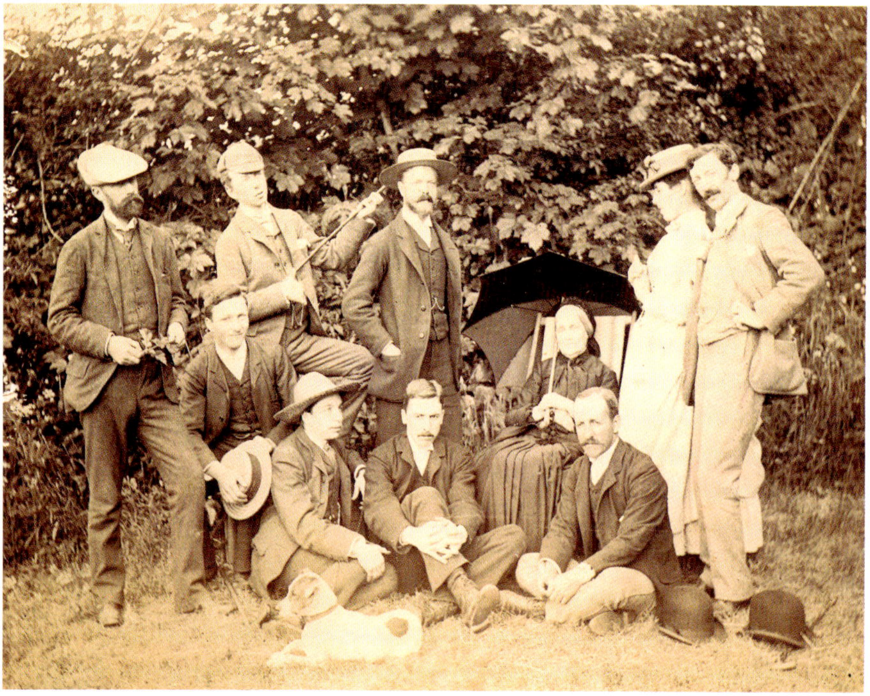

58
Photo of Newlyn group of artists with Elizabeth Forbes and Mrs Forbes. Stanhope Forbes is standing beside his wife. Standing from left to right are Garstin, Bodilly and Millard. Seated on the grass from left to right are not known, Chevallier Tayler and Bourdillon. (Penlee House Gallery and Museum, on loan from the Cornwall Centre)

3 The Legacy of Forbes and the Next Generation

Two events occurred in the 1890s which consolidated the position of the Newlyn artists as a definite group – one was the founding of the Newlyn Art Gallery in 1895 and the other the decision by Stanhope and Elizabeth Forbes in 1899 to open a school of painting, which brought the next generation of artists to Newlyn and Lamorna.

By 1895, the Newlyn artists were exhibiting regularly in London at the Royal Academy and at the New English Art Club, but other than the private views in their own studios and the odd exhibition at the Penzance Art Society and the Royal Cornwall Polytechnic Society, there was little or no opportunity for the artists to exhibit in Cornwall. It was a growing interest in the Newlyn painters from the outside and a push from the artists themselves that instigated the idea of an art gallery in Newlyn. The building of the Newlyn Art Gallery, which opened on 22 October 1895, is a lasting legacy of Forbes and the original members of the Newlyn colony of artists. Forbes and fellow artists Bramley, Gotch and Langley approached the philanthropist Passmore Edwards who also commissioned public libraries and hospitals throughout Cornwall. Charles Le Grice donated the land on which the gallery was built and the Newlyn Society of Artists was formed; it continues to this day.

Forbes was clear that the Gallery was not a club for the artists but a building for the public's benefit and use. The intention was to fund the gallery with donations from subscribers either as donors who paid no less than 10 guineas which allowed them two tickets for all the exhibitions and private views, or as fellows who paid one guinea annually in advance for the same privileges. There was an entrance fee for everyone else of 6 pence for exhibitions and a shilling on private view days. They also intended to rent the gallery out for dances and other events and to charge a commission on the sales of work.

The inaugural exhibition showed over 141 works and 23 paintings were sold. The Society was organized with a chairman, the first being Gotch. There was an executive committee made up of six members with an honorary secretary, the first being Percy Craft. Over the years the Newlyn Art Gallery became the focus for the artists living and working in and round Newlyn as the exhibitions were used as previews before their work went to London to be shown at the Royal Academy.

However, despite these new opportunities for the artists to exhibit in Cornwall, by 1899 many of the original Newlyners began to leave for other parts of the country. Fred Hall left in 1898; Chevallier Tayler left for London in 1895 where he continued to paint mainly society paintings. Ralph Todd did not leave Cornwall, but in the 1890s moved to St Keverne and then Helston. In 1895, Frank Bramley left for Droitwich in the Midlands and later settled in Grasmere in Westmoreland. To attract new and younger artists to Newlyn, Elizabeth and Stanhope Forbes decided to open a school of painting, which they would run jointly. Thus in October 1899 the doors opened to the Forbes' School of Painting and Drawing. The teaching was undertaken in the studios in the meadow with the emphasis being on outdoor painting.

Gladys Beattie Crozier wrote several articles in 'Everywoman's Encyclopaedia' about the school. 'The course of study in the studios consists mainly of drawing and painting from life. On Mondays, Wednesdays and Fridays students work from 9.30–12.30 and again from 2–5 from models posed in the studios. On the three alternate days they are expected to work indoors during the morning only, and during the afternoon they are free to work out of doors. When the weather is favourable the study of figure painting is carried on in the studio garden.'[27] Elizabeth Forbes encouraged students to be interested in painting costumed figures outdoors as Gladys Crozier relates in another article. 'I found two girls who were enthusiastically at work upon a somewhat ambitious attempt to portray a crimson robed enchantress lying hidden in a wood....the model, garbed in one of Mrs. Stanhope Forbes' pet mediaeval Italian garments, bore an air of magic and enchantment'.[28] Elizabeth had many pupils at the school of painting one of which was Wynifrid Tennyson Jesse, nicknamed 'Fryniwyd' or 'Fryn' for short. Her account of a day at the Forbes' school of painting describes it as a tough one for the students. They were expected to have cleaned the studios, rubbed the floors with French chalk and draped the models' chairs and have made sandwiches before 9 o'clock when Elizabeth Forbes arrived to start teaching. She was also in charge of organising the evening entertainment for all the students, which included concerts, plays, parties and dances.

Stanhope Forbes outlined their philosophy of the teaching at the school in a lecture on the school's first day, 'My wife and I, in this opening term of our school, have thought it advisable to lead you all to devote your energies mainly to the study of drawing. It may seem scarcely so amusing as splashing about with a paint-box, but the qualities which go to produce a satisfactory charcoal drawing are well-nigh indispensable, and moreover the foundation upon which the best work rests.'[29]

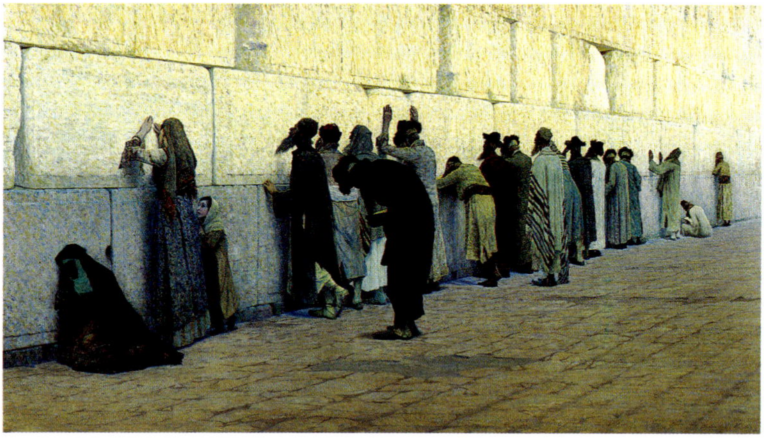

There was no entrance exam to get into the school but students had to send examples of their work in advance to show they were sufficiently proficient. The fees were for the summer term £10.10s and for the winter term £12.12s but students could join in at anytime for £3.3s per month. The fees included the use of the models, the studios and easels. Students had to provide their own paints and canvases.

Hundreds of artists went through the school over the next 50 years, while other artists such as George Sherwood Hunter (1846–1919) who came to live in The Malt House in Newlyn in 1902, helped the Forbes. In Mrs Lionel Birch's biography of Stanhope and Elizabeth Forbes, she pays tribute to Hunter who is described as 'an artist of sincere and thoughtful individuality who is always ready to help and supplement the teacher's efforts. His own studio... is a perfect treasure house of beautiful and interesting work. His pictures are rarely seen in exhibitions – for he loves to keep them about him.'[30] His studio was also in Bateman's Meadow, from which he painted many views of Mount's Bay. He is not well known as a Newlyn painter and travelled a great deal, hence his frequent foreign subject matter. A *Place of Wailing* (1910/11) (Plymouth) is a typical example.

Another artist who taught at the Forbes' school was Mr Lionel Lea Townley Birch (1858–1930) from Bramshall in Staffordshire, not to be confused with J Samuel 'Lamorna' Birch (1869–1955) who developed another colony of artists further down the coast at Lamorna. By the turn of the century, further new approaches to painting had filtered through from the continent and were reflected in the next generation of Newlyn and Lamorna artists.

Many of the students who came to Cornwall to study at the Forbes' school later decided to stay; many moved to Lamorna Valley. Many of the students who met at Newlyn married. This produced a social circle of painter couples influencing each other's artistic practice. The difference between the first and second generation of artist couples at Newlyn was that more of the women in the second generation partnerships were artists or like Gertrude Harvey, became artists. Elizabeth Forbes and Caroline Gotch were the noticeable exceptions to the rule in the first generation; they were both women artists who married other artists of an equal standing. The fact that by the 1900s this had become the norm reflected the change in times and the greater opportunities for women to train and become professional artists. In some cases, the women, for example, Dod Procter and Laura Knight,

59
Sherwood Hunter
A Place of Wailing
oil on canvas
102.5x183.5cm
(Plymouth City Museum and Art Gallery)

60
Newlyn Copper
(Penlee House Gallery and Museum)
Photography by Steve Tanner

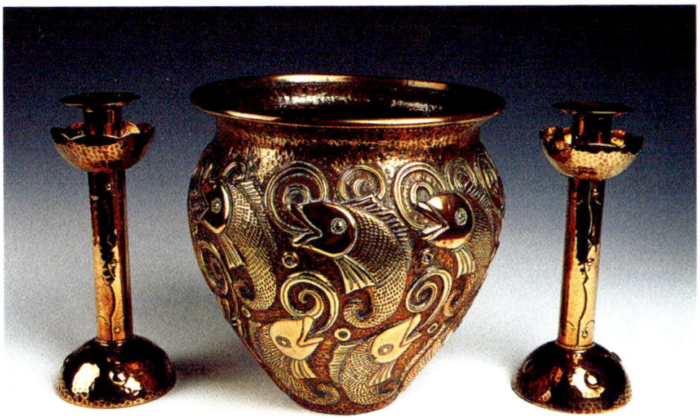

61
Stanhope Forbes
The Young Apprentice, Newlyn Copperworks c1908
oil on canvas
76.5x61.5cm
(Penlee House Gallery and Museum)
© Courtesy of the artist's estate/ Bridgeman Art Library

went on to become more famous and to be regarded as more important artists than their husbands.

The Newlyn artists were sympathetic to the vagaries of the fishing industry and did what they could to help the community. The fishing industry was always in flux, depending on weather, the size of the shoals each year and the state of the market. By the end of the 1880s unemployment amongst fishermen especially the young was more prevalent. It was through the efforts of Newlyn artists Percy Craft, Thomas Gotch, JD MacKenzie (1861–1918) and Reginald Dick (1868–1941), that a craft workshop was set up in Newlyn to offer new skills. It was supported financially by the local benefactor TB Bolitho. The first courses at the Newlyn Industrial Class, or the copperworks as it became known locally, were in metalwork, enameling and embroidery and were held in an old fish loft at the top of Champions Slip. Out of all the artists it was JD MacKenzie who played the greatest role in directing the workshop from 1890 until his death in the First World War. Stanhope Forbes' painting *The Young Apprentice, Newlyn Copperworks* (c1908) (Penlee) depicts MacKenzie watching over a young lad whilst studying the art of repoussé copper beating. But even MacKenzie accepted he did not have all the necessary skills to teach the more elaborate procedures of some of the crafts and so persuaded the master craftsman John Pearson (1858–1930) to come down from London in 1892 to teach at the Newlyn Industrial Class. One of the first most prominent commissions for the Industrial Class was to make four beaten copper panels for Newlyn Art Gallery when it opened in 1895. The panels were designed by JD MacKenzie and Thomas Gotch and illustrated the four elements earth, air, fire and water. They were made by Philip Hodder (dates unknown), who was one of the students of copperwork from the Industrial Class. This work and the regular exhibitions held at the Home Art and Industrial Association at the Albert Hall in 1899, 1900 and 1902 demonstrated the high standards the Newlyn metal craftsmen achieved. The Newlyn metal industry came to an end during the First World War but was later revived in the 1920s on a more commercial basis. It was finally killed by competition from cheap foreign imports.

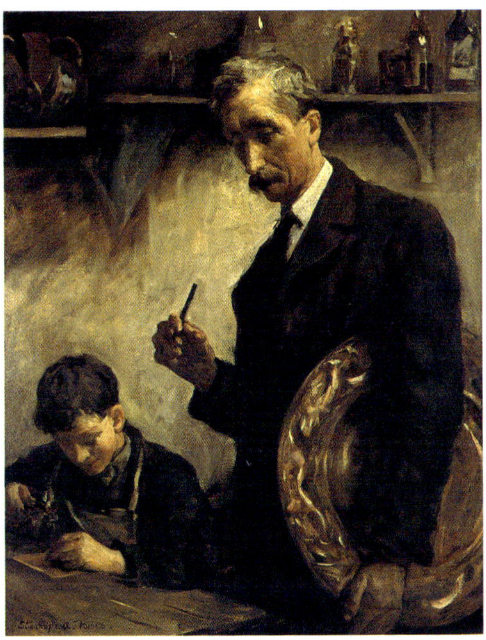

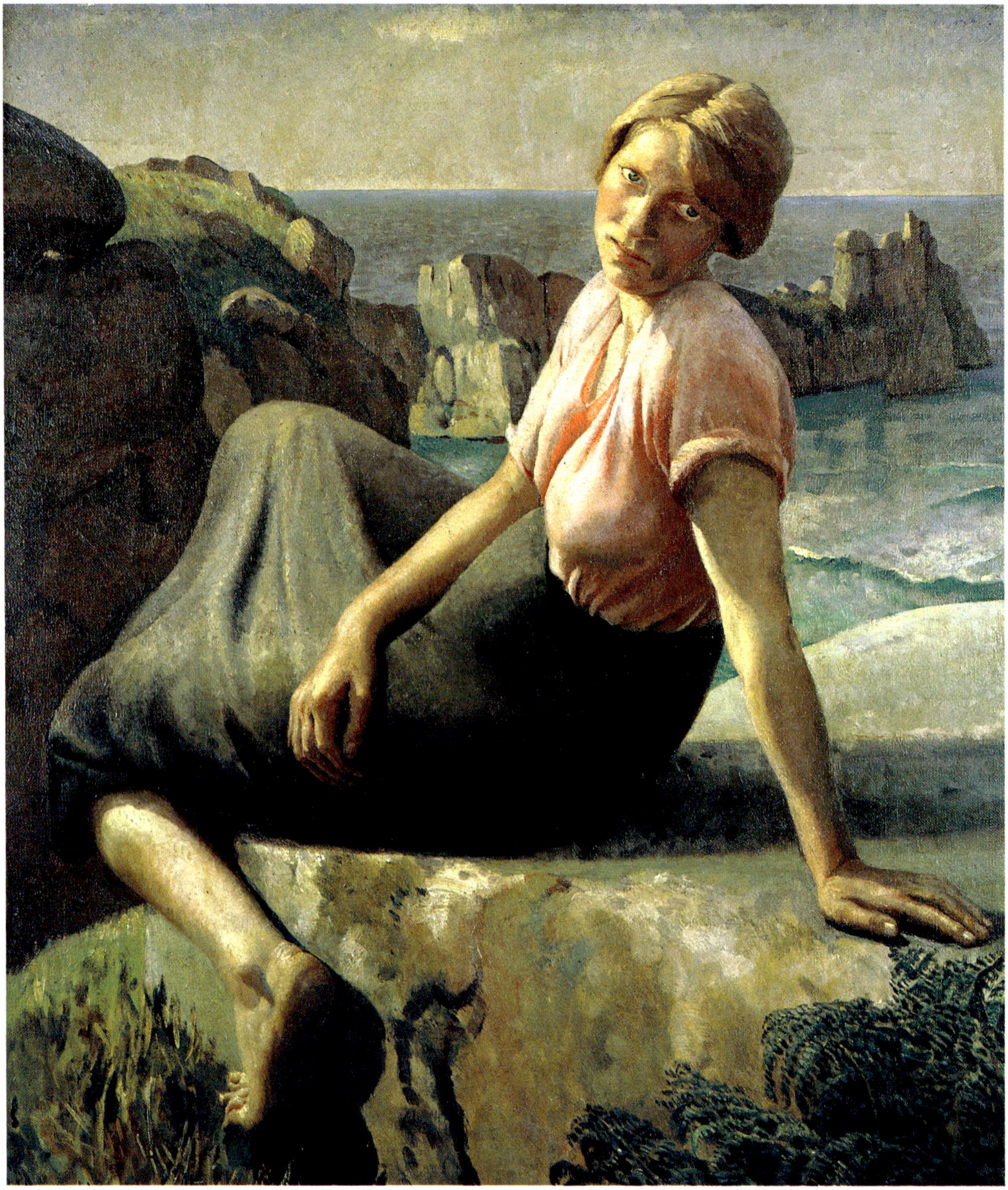

61
Harold Harvey
Girl on a Cliff 1926
oil on canvas
101.5x89cm
(Penlee House Gallery and Museum, on loan from a Private Collection)
© Courtesy of the artist's estate/ Bridgeman Art Library

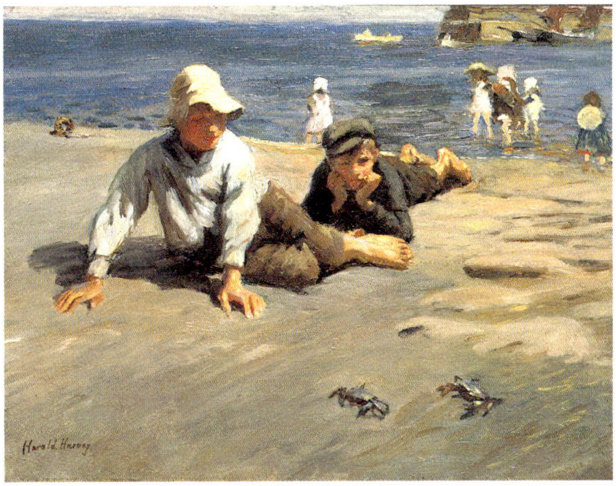

62
Harold Harvey
Sport on the Shore, a Crab Race
oil on canvas
30.5x40.5cm
(Plymouth City Museum and Art Gallery)
© Courtesy of the artist's estate/ Bridgeman Art Library

Harold Harvey (1874–1941) and Gertrude Harvey (née Bodinnar) (1879–1966)

Harold Harvey was a Penzance boy who became a painter. His work typifies the changing styles of the Newlyn and Lamorna painters and of Cornish life. He was a pupil of Norman Garstin, who ran painting and drawing courses at the turn of the century which were advertised alongside the Forbes' school of painting. One of Harvey's earliest works to have survived is *Sport on the Shore, a Crab Race* (Plymouth), thought to date from about 1890 when Harvey was just 16 years old. He came from a wealthy middle class family who did not approve of their eldest son painting for a living. Born in North Parade, Penzance on 29th May 1874, he was one of the eight children of Francis and Mary Harvey. Francis was general manager of Carne and Carne's Banking Co Ltd.

Harvey was clearly influenced by Garstin in both his philosophy of art and in his practice. Garstin wrote 'my chief theory on painting is not to have a theory, painting is purely a personal matter; I don't know how different people see nature, but certainly in passing through their consciousness it is bound to be transmitted absolutely different.' Garstin goes on to say that modern painting appealed to him and 'the experiments that young men make.'[31] Harvey went on to study in Paris for two years, 1894–1896, at the Académie Julian and at the atelier Colarossi as well as the atelier of Auguste-Joseph Deleclusse.

On his return to Newlyn, Harvey exhibited regularly at the Newlyn Art Gallery and in 1898 had his first picture accepted at the Royal Academy. Although Harvey did not study directly with Forbes, he was clearly influenced by the old style of Newlyn painting as seen in his painting *Newlyn Harbour* (1907) (Plymouth).

Many of his paintings were rural scenes of farm workers in the fields, or crossing streams as well as children playing by the sea or in the countryside. Harvey socialized with many of the students at the Forbes' school, attending their functions held in the studios and it was here that Harvey probably encountered his future wife Gertrude Bodinnar, from Newlyn.

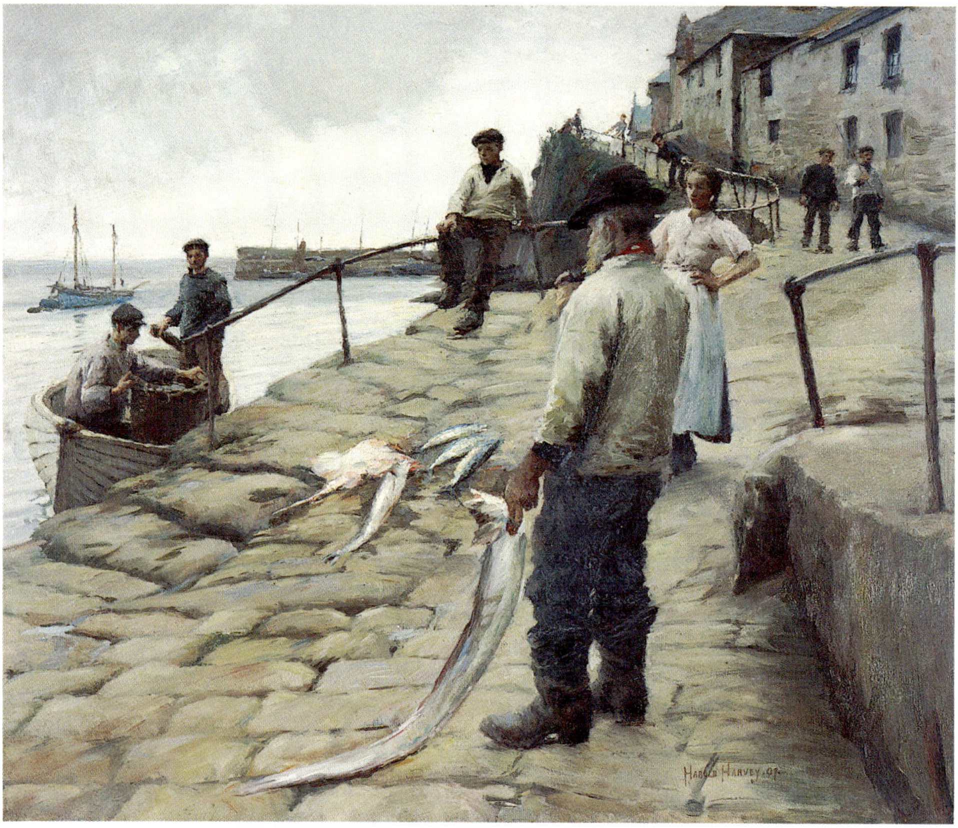

63
Harold Harvey
Newlyn Harbour
1907
oil on canvas
63.5x76.5cm
(Plymouth City Museum and Art Gallery Loan Collection)
© Courtesy of the artist's estate/ Bridgeman Art Library

64
Harold Harvey
St Just Tin Miners
1935
oil on canvas
(Royal Cornwall Museum, Truro)
© Courtesy of the artist's estate/ Bridgeman Art Library

She was a model for the artists at the Forbes' school and later took up painting herself. She became the inspiration for many of Harvey's later works. They married in 1911 and established a home at Maen Cottage in Newlyn. The kitchen of the cottage featured in many of Harvey's paintings, with its Cornish dresser covered in pottery.

In the 1920s and 30s Harold Harvey undertook several paintings of the industrial landscape of Cornwall in particular the china clay pits at Leswidden and the tin mines. This side of Cornish life was very rarely used as subject matter by Newlyn and Lamorna artists. Ironically in the painting *St Just Tin Miners* (1935) (Royal Cornwall Museum), the two men in the foreground, Nicholas Grenfell and Sydney Angove, both local tin miners who had worked at Botallack and Geevor, are depicted in front of a Malayan tin mine. In the late 1920s it was the cheaper tin supplied from Malaya that undercut the price of Cornish tin and many miners were forced to emigrate in search of work.

Gertrude Harvey was mainly known for her flower paintings. She exhibited at the Royal Academy where she showed twenty paintings from 1930–1949. She also painted landscapes which were shown at the Newlyn Art Gallery and in joint exhibitions held with Harold at the Leicester Gallery in 1918 and in 1920. Gertrude Harvey and the other women artists of the colony were recurrent models in Harvey's paintings of the 1920s. He came into his own with a genre of pictures of women often dressed in the fashion of the day. The loving way in which he painted his wife in her bedroom or in the kitchen is touching. They

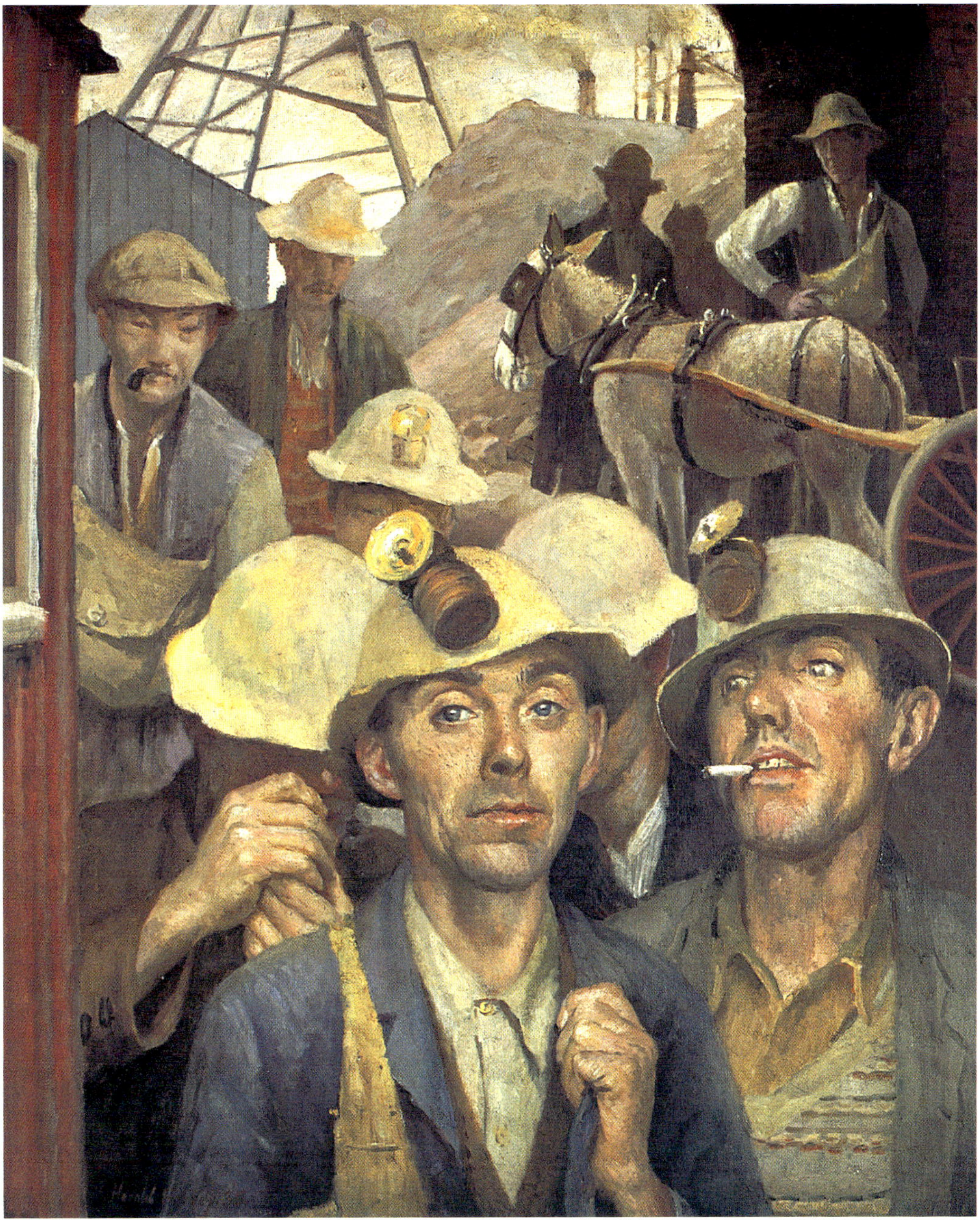

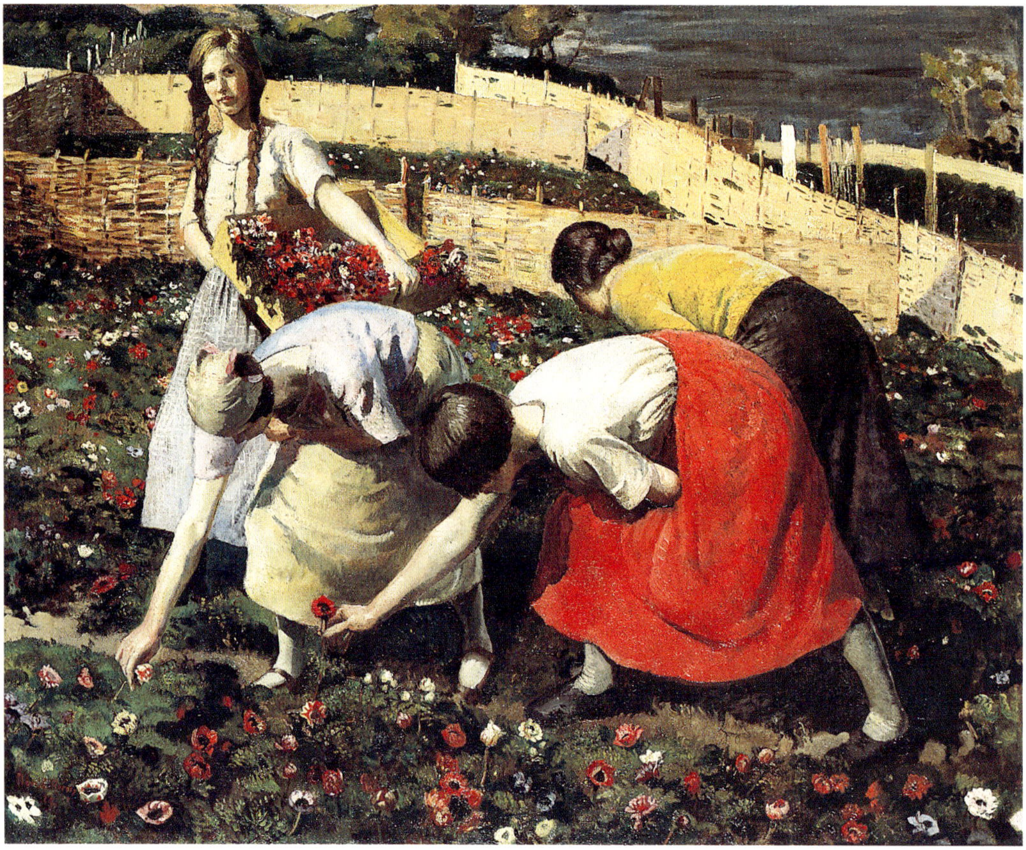

are controlled paintings, which pay homage to Dutch interiors with frequent use of black and white diamond tiles on the floor similar to Vermeer's interiors. Harvey was greatly influenced in the early 20s by fellow artists and friends, the Procters and the Knights. His painting *Girl on a Cliff* (1926) (Penlee) shows a figure painted in a very sculptural way which is similar to Ernest and Dod Procter's paintings of the time. It was Harvey's joyous use of bright colours as seen in *The Donkey Meadow* (1924) (Private Collection) which made his work very decorative and successful. Harold Harvey and Ernest Procter set up their own painting school in a large studio near Newlyn harbour in 1920. It was advertised as 'A New School, Harold Harvey and Ernest Procter, Newlyn. Figure, Still Life, Landscape; Open all year; oil and watercolour.'

Harvey converted to Catholicism in 1926, possibly due to the influence of his friend the Reverend Bernard Walke who was the Catholic Anglican vicar of the church at St Hilary. He painted several works on religious themes including *The Flight* (1925) (Private Collection), *Madonna of the Bridges* (1930) (Private Collection), *A May Procession* (1935) (Private Collection) and *Ancilla Domini* (1938) (whereabouts unknown). Although he never received as much acclaim as some of his fellow Newlyners, Harold Harvey had considerable success as an exhibiting artist and showed his work every year between 1931 and 1941 at the Royal Academy. He also exhibited frequently at the Royal Hibernian Academy in Dublin, as well as the Royal Scottish Academy in 1920, the Royal Glasgow Institute, 1933 and 1941 and four years at the Pittsburgh Carnegie Institute in America from 1933–1936.

65
Harold Harvey *The Donkey Meadow* 1924 oil on canvas 60x75cm (Private Collection) © Courtesy of the artist's estate/ Bridgeman Art Library

66
Alec Walker *Men Working in the Violet Fields at Trembath* 1927 watercolour 61.6x73cm (Penlee House Gallery and Museum)

67
Alec Walker *Crysède Cherry Tree design* date unknown silk (Penlee House Gallery and Museum)

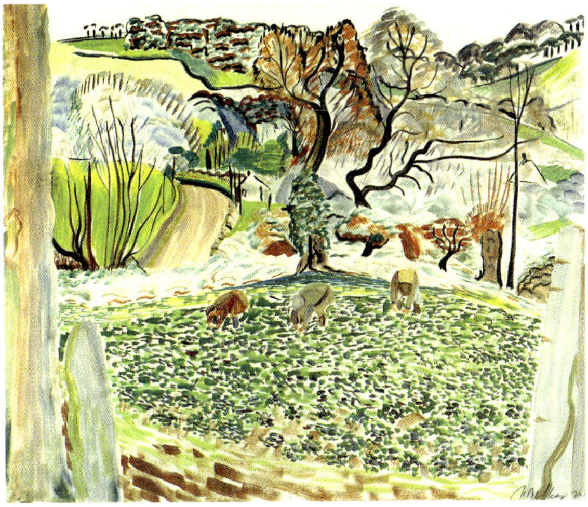

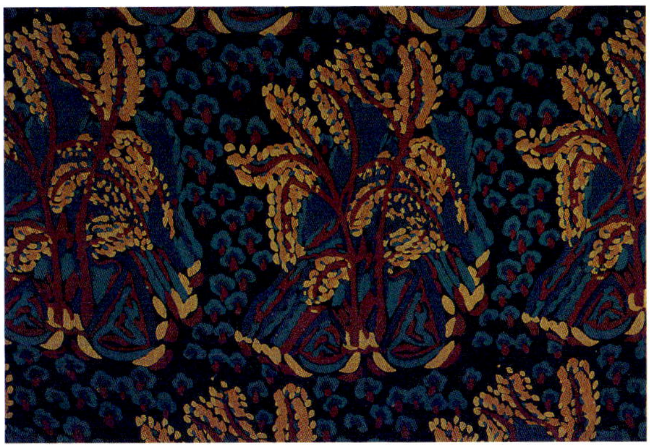

Alec Walker (1889–1964) and Crysède

In the 1920s as the fishing industry dwindled, Newlyn saw a revival in the copper crafts. The arrival of the Yorkshire textile designer Alec Walker created another craft industry for Newlyn in the form of his unique range of handprinted textiles known as 'Crysède'. Walker first heard of Newlyn through his future wife Kathleen (Kay) Earle who had studied at the Forbes' school of painting in 1910 and was a keen designer herself. Walker and Kay married in 1918 and moved to Newlyn to set up the Crysède silk works in a converted row of derelict fishing cottages. They lived at Myrtle Cottage, once home to a group of women students at the Forbes' school, known as the Myrtage.

Walker's Crysède designs were made on raw silk which had been bleached and dyed, then hand block printed. His designs were influenced by the friendship and encouragement of modernist artists, such as Raoul Dufy, Wyndham Lewis and McKnight Kauffer in the dynamism of their composition and possibly in the use of bold and vibrant colour; the subjects were mainly based on his own drawings and paintings of the Cornish landscape. His patterns were made up into dresses, coats, skirts, blouses, scarves and handkerchiefs which were sold through shops from Penzance to Edinburgh and through mail order to Paris, New York and Australia. The Walkers were great friends with the Harveys and many of Harold Harvey's paintings include his wife and women friends wearing Crysède textiles.

The business expanded in 1925 when Tom Heron, father of Patrick Heron, (later to be a leading St Ives artist), a silk importer and clothes manufacturer from Walker's Yorkshire days, joined the business. The premises moved to the Island, St Ives in 1926 and remained until 1941, but Walker and Heron had left by 1929 after Walker suffered a nervous breakdown and Heron went to Welwyn Garden City where he set up his own successful 'Cresta' textiles company. Walker continued to paint and exhibited his work in London and returned briefly to designing for Crysède in 1931–3 but stopped when running a beef cattle farm in Yorkshire took precedence. After the Second World War he returned to Cornwall to live in Falmouth where he died in 1964.

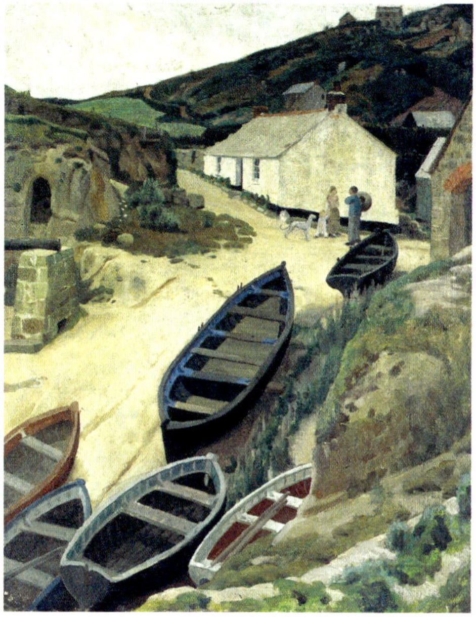

68
Ernest Procter
Porthgwarra
date unknown
oil on canvas
66.2x50cm
(Penlee House Gallery and Museum, on loan from Private Collection)

69
Dod Procter
Portrait of Eileen Mayo
date unknown
oil on canvas
77.5x66.5cm
(Penlee House Gallery and Museum, on loan from Private Collection)

Ernest Procter (1886–1935) and Dod Procter (née Shaw) (1892–1972)

Ernest Procter was born in Tynemouth but was brought up near Leeds where his father was a professor. He came to study at the Forbes' school of painting in 1907 where he was seen to be a very good student. He also went to the atelier Colarossi in Paris. At the beginning of the First World War Ernest Procter declared himself a conscientious objector, joined the Red Cross and served in France as part of the Friends Ambulance Unit. He helped the wounded, kept the ambulances working and even helped the local farmers bring in their harvest. At the end of the war he gained permission to record the work of the Red Cross as an official war artist; six watercolours were bought for the Imperial War Museum. On his return to Newlyn, Ernest Procter and Harold Harvey set up their own small painting school. His students included Dorcie Sykes (1908–1998), the daughter of John Guttridge Sykes (1866–1941), Midge Bruford (1902–1958) and Billie Waters (1896–1979), who also modelled for Ernest.

There are several different aspects of Ernest Procter's work: his sketches, often in watercolour, done from nature on the spot; *plein air* paintings that were often of beach scenes with figures like *Porthgwarra* (date unknown) (Penlee); mystical figure pictures — these are very decorative images that involve the use of figures and animals as allegories, such as *Young Witches at Play in the Night Sky* (date unknown) (Private Collection); his religious pictures such as the commissions for the church at St Hilary.

In the 1920s there were times when Ernest and Dod Procter's pictures became very similar

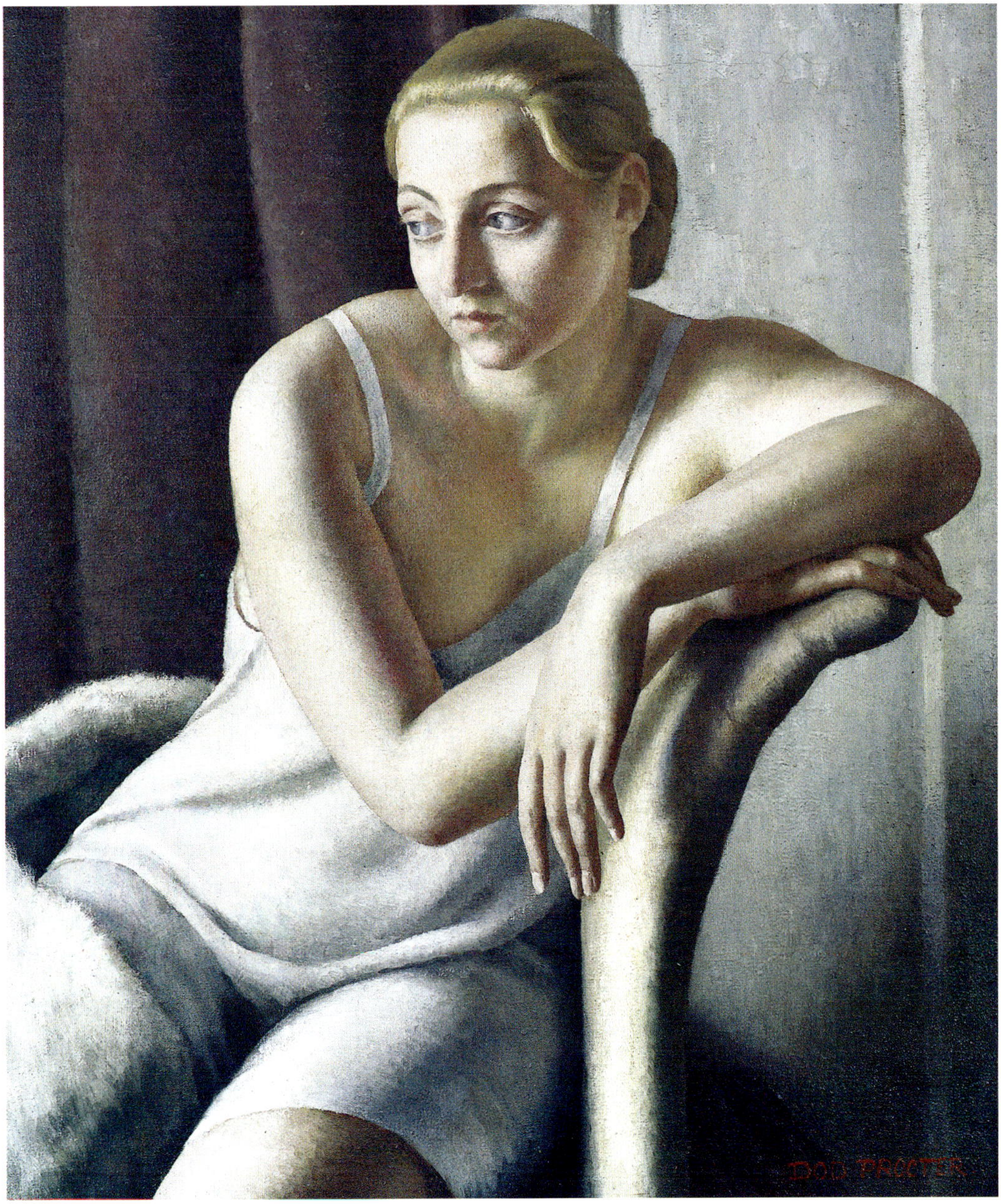
DOD PROCTER

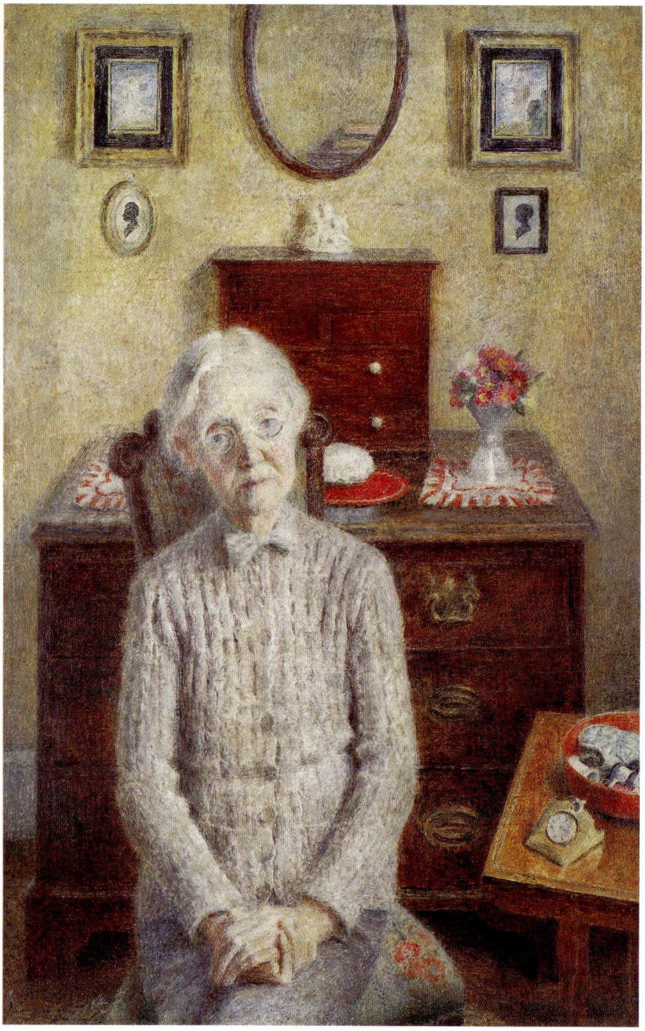

in form with large, monumental female figures dominating the canvas. An unusual commission to decorate a palace belonging to a wealthy Chinese merchant in Rangoon, Burma, which they received in 1919, could have influenced this style of painting. They painted murals for the walls on a salary of £100 a month with a house and a car. However, things did not turn out as planned as the merchant did not think the paintings would last so only paid them £20 a month and they had to find their own accommodation. They made ends meet by painting portraits of both local people and members of the British colonial establishment. This artist couple must have seen the huge Buddhist sculptures in Burma which possibly inspired the strong sculptural quality in their work.

Dod Procter was a good-looking girl, Laura Knight described her as 'a charming young thing, with a brilliant complexion, enormous dark eyes and long slim legs — swift and active as a gazelle' [32] It was whilst studying at Newlyn that she met Ernest Procter. In 1910 Mrs Shaw accompanied her daughter to Paris to study at the atelier Colarossi looking at paintings by the Impressionists, Post-Impressionists, Cézanne and Renoir. These artists were to have a big affect on Dod as a painter which is evident in her later work.

Dod Procter in many ways outshone her husband as a painter. This may have been due to her unusually early start in painting at the age of 15 when she enrolled in the Forbes' school of painting. The fact that her mother decided to leave London after her husband died and chose Newlyn as the place to bring up her young family was fortuitous for Dod. They lived at Myrtle Cottage, which in fact was a large Georgian town house and it was shared with lodgers who were other young ladies studying at the Forbes' school.

On her return from Paris in 1912, she and Ernest were married in Paul church. Dod Procter took a long time to recover from the birth of their only child, Bill, in 1913. But, in the same

70
Dod Procter
Aunt Lilla 1943
oil on canvas
105.8x68.8cm
(Penlee House Gallery and Museum, on loan from Private Collection)

year she showed her first painting at the Royal Academy. In the early days of exhibiting she mainly showed flower subjects. However, by 1919, the Procters were being reviewed in the art magazines of the day as 'modern' painters. Dod Procter's work was described as giving 'the impression of great skill, deep honesty and careful, perhaps overcareful, deliberation.'[33] The trip to Rangoon in Burma with Ernest in August was to be a great influence in formalizing her style. The sculptural qualities of her figure paintings in the 1920s are testament to this.

On her return to Newlyn in 1921/2 Dod Procter focused on painting mainly single figures, some nudes, others clothed portraits. Her paintings such as *Model* (1925) (whereabouts unknown) and *Model Resting* (1924) (whereabouts unknown) were shown at the Royal Academy to great acclaim. She often used the same models as Laura Knight; they were brought down to Newlyn from London. Later Dod Procter started to use local girls in her portraits. The friendship between Laura Knight and Dod Procter and their influence on each other was strong. Dod Procter was probably unusual in that she was one of the few women artists to influence Laura Knight. In her paintings of nudes Dod Procter was demonstrating the essence of her art in their monumentality and simplicity of form. Her paintings show the human form without sentimentality. The colours she used in these paintings are very muted adding to the feeling of their being carved out of stone as can be seen in *Eileen Mayo* (date unknown) (Penlee).

It was Dod Procter's large portrait of the local fisherman's daughter Cissie Barnes which when shown at the Royal Academy in the spring of 1927, catapulted her into the art history books. This painting, *Morning* (Tate Gallery), was bought by the 'Daily Mail' for the nation. the 'Daily Mail's' coverage of the painting and the artist made Dod Procter famous. Her painting *Virginal* (1929) (Private Collection) of a nude holding a dove gave her equal fame but for different reasons; it was rejected by the Royal Academy and shown at the Leicester Gallery instead, where people flocked to see it.

The Procters joined the New English Art Club in 1929 and showed regularly at its galleries. Dod Procter also had exhibitions at the Leicester Gallery in 1932, 1942 and 1945. She was elected an Associate Royal Academician in 1934, the third woman in the Academy's history to achieve such a position. She was made a Royal Academician in 1942. They took a flat in London in the early 30s, which they visited every year until Ernest's death in 1935.

Dod Procter travelled to America and Canada in 1936 where her work had previously been exhibited. She continued to paint figures and still lifes in the 30s but moved to painting landscapes and painting outdoors. In 1938 she took a house in Zennor and became friends with and was influenced by Alethea Garstin. Her technique noticeably changed at this time to a much looser style of applying the paint. Her figures were portrayed more softly using an impressionistic technique, which made them less monumental and sculptural, and more atmospheric, such as *Aunt Lilla* (1943) Penlee).

She travelled to Africa and Jamaica in the 1950s painting children as her main subject. An example of one of her paintings at this time is *African Head* (date unknown) (Plymouth). Back in Newlyn she continued to paint still lifes and sent her pictures regularly for show at the Royal Academy. Sadly she did not see a retrospective of her work there before she died.

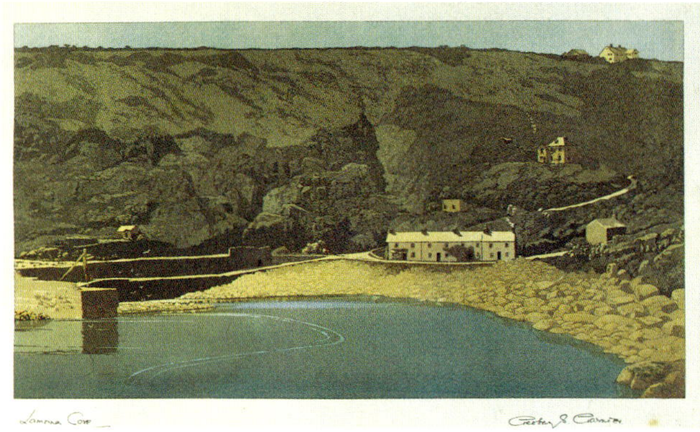

Geoffrey Sneyd Garnier (1889–1970) and Jill W Garnier (née Blyth) (1890–1966)

Geoffrey Garnier came to study at the Forbes' school of painting in 1912 after studying at Herkomers' school of art in Bushey. Art had not been his first choice of career as he originally trained as an engineer in Toronto, Canada. He had also spent time prospecting for gold in the Yukon. In Newlyn, Garnier stayed at Trewarveneth Farm where Stanhope and Elizabeth Forbes had lived. Whilst studying at the Forbes' school of painting, Geoffrey met Jill Blyth, his first cousin, who was also an artist. They married in 1917, honeymooning at Orchard Cottage which later became their family home. With his previous background of engineering, Garnier was drawn to the art of etching and in particular colour aquatints; he was a natural etcher and could draw straight on to the copper plate without doing any preliminary designs.[34] He drew many subjects including local buildings, and coastal views such as *Lamorna Cove* (date unknown) (Penlee). He had a great fondness for cars and all kinds of machinery; he was also a writer and bookbinder.

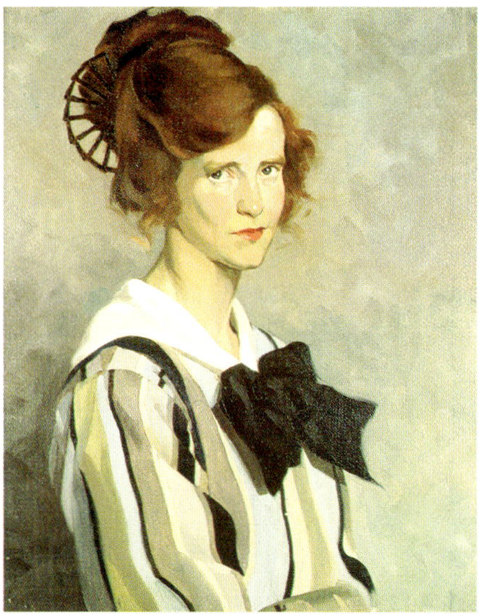

Jill Blyth was born at Quidenham in Norfolk and educated at Cheltenham Ladies College. The influence of Stanhope Forbes' teaching is very evident in her portraits, which have been regarded as her strongest work. She exhibited at the Royal Academy and the Royal West of England Academy. As her son, Peter, wrote of his mother: 'It is sad that so gifted an artist should have had to work only part-time, while running a house, bringing up a family and generally being a wife and mother.'[35] He also commented that her husband as a painter rather unjustly overshadowed her. She was an accomplished needlewoman as well and produced exquisite silk stitched pictures.

71
Geoffrey Sneyd Garnier
Lamorna Cove
date unknown
aquatint
25x46.4cm
(Penlee House Gallery and Museum)

72
Jill Garnier
Sarah Kitchen
date unknown
oil on canvas
60x50cm (Private Collection)

73
Charles Simpson
The Line Fishing Season St Ives
date unknown
oil on canvas
101.7x123cm
(Plymouth City Museum and Art Gallery)

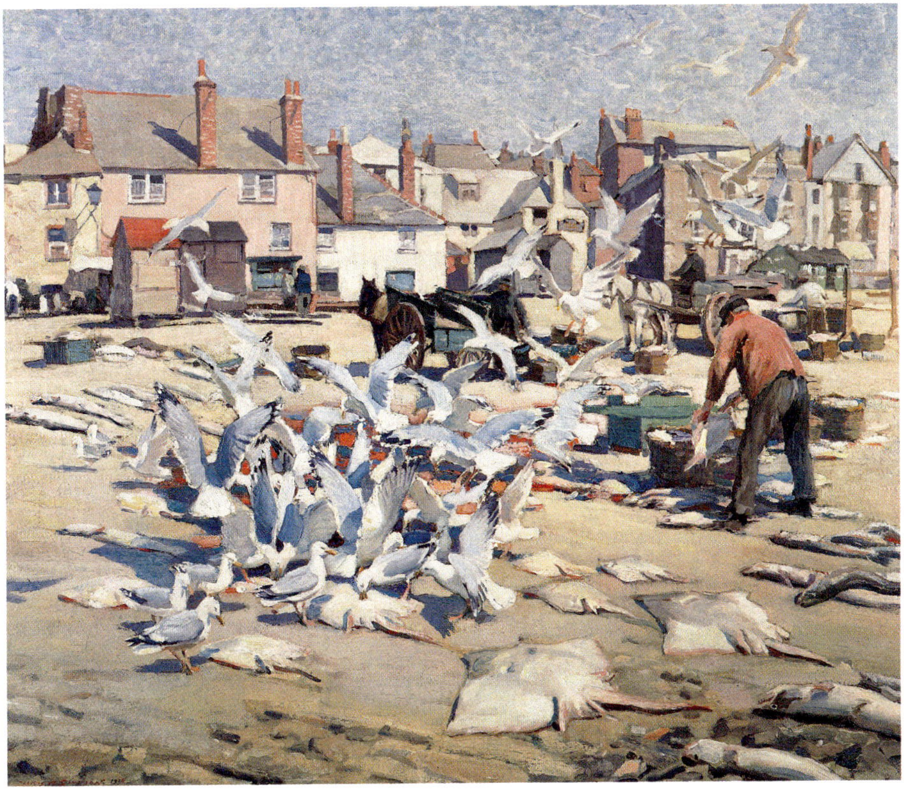

Charles Simpson (1885–1971) and Ruth Simpson (née Alison) (1889–1964)

Another dynamic young couple who met at the Forbes' school and went on to set up their own school of painting in St Ives were the Simpsons. Ruth Alison studied under Stanhope Forbes in Newlyn in 1911–12, where she met Charles Simpson; they married in 1913. They lived briefly in Lamorna where Leonora, their daughter, was born. Ruth Simpson was mainly known as a portrait painter and her oil called *Maroon and Gold* (date unknown) (Penlee), painted before she married Charles Simpson, shows her skill in this area. Although taught by Forbes, Ruth Simpson developed her own style of portraiture. The lighting on her sitters is not as dramatic as in Forbes' portraits. Instead, she used colour in a more modern way with bright coloured backgrounds for her sitters as opposed to the more conventional 19th century dark background. The very title implies a reference to Whistler and his use of painting titles made up of the predominant colours in them. The fact that she and Charles Simpson left Lamorna for St Ives, where the artistic colony had greater interest in Modernism and the aesthetics of painting, reflects their own interests in these aspects of art. Ruth Simpson painted several of her fellow women artists including Ella Naper and Gertrude Harvey. She exhibited her work at the Society of Women Artists

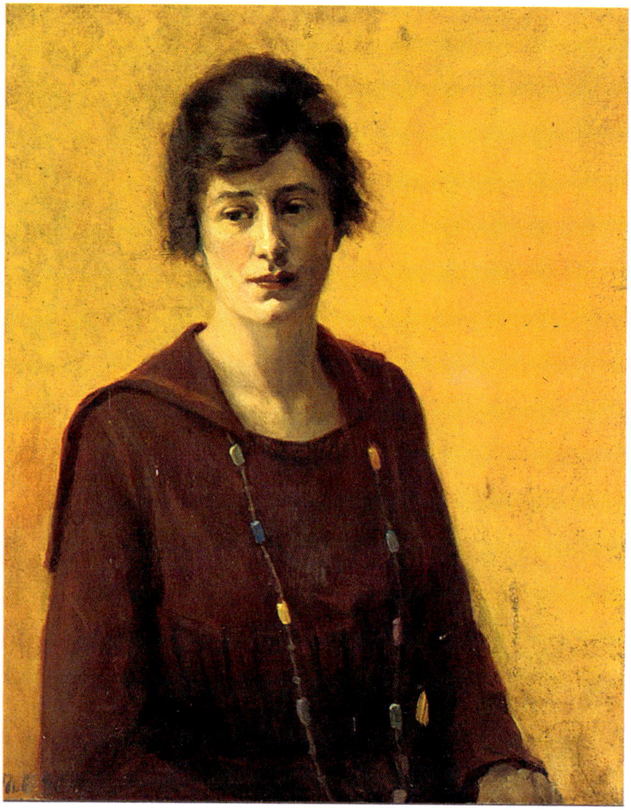

and the Royal Academy. She and her family moved to London in 1924 but returned to live in Lamorna in 1931.

Charles Simpson was born in Camberley and came from a military background. His career in the army was cut short by a riding accident: in 1905 he came to Newlyn. He studied art for a short while at Bushey under the animal painter Lucy Kemp Welch. Animals and birds were his forté as an artist. He was also friends with and studied under someone whom he regarded as the best painters of horses at the time, Alfred Munnings (1878–1959). It was Simpson who encouraged Munnings to come to Cornwall in 1908. Charles was not at the Forbes' school but was taught by the St Ives artist John Noble Barlow (1861–1917). Even so his early paintings, such as *An Autumn Sunset* (1913) (whereabouts unknown), show a distinct influence of Stanhope Forbes' later pastoral paintings with their strong lighting effects. Charles Simpson had also studied at Julian's atelier, had observed Impressionism and was clearly influenced by it. When he met Ruth Alison, she thought he was a talented artist. 'He is awfully clever and has a picture of ducks on the line at the Royal Academy this year. He had another wonderful, huge moorland picture accepted… He is quite young too — only 28 and is doing a marvellous 8ft canvas of life sized seagulls and sunny cliffs.'[36] He had another fan of his early work in Laura Knight who also liked painting on a big scale.

The Simpsons whilst in Newlyn were great friends with Harold Harvey and his wife Gertrude; Simpson's woodblock illustrations in 'The Paper Chase' of 1909, show the influence of Harvey's work. The painting *Penzance from Newlyn* (1914) (Penlee) shows Simpson depicting a scene in dark gloomy colours, but this was all to change when he and his wife and daughter Leonora moved to St Ives. A touching, boldly executed portrait of Leonora called *The Pergola* (1924) (Royal Cornwall Museum) has a palette which is very bright, reflecting a sunny day in the garden where the picture was clearly painted. It also shows Simpson's shift in style to a more impressionistic one.

The Simpsons moved to St Ives in 1916, and set up their school of painting which was advertised as covering 'all branches of painting and drawing and especially modern methods of handling oils, tempera, watercolour etc and illustration work with a view to

74
Ruth Simpson
Maroon and Gold
date unknown
oil on canvas
61.3x50.6cm
(Penlee House Gallery and Museum, on loan from Newlyn Art Gallery)

75
Charles Simpson
The Western Union Fleet (Mounts Bay)
1949
oil on canvas
91.3x145cm
(Penlee House Gallery and Museum)

reproduction.'[37] The subjects were often similar to the early Newlyn School paintings such as *The Line Fishing Season, St Ives* (date unknown) (Plymouth) where the fish are laid out on the beach with the horse and carts on the beach waiting to be filled with the catch. That is the only similarity as Charles Simpson used the subject as an excuse to paint a rich tapestry of colours created by a flock of seagulls landing on the beach picking over the fish.

It was pressure to paint his more popular hunting scenes that took Charles and Ruth Simpson to London in 1924. Whilst there Charles encountered the visiting rodeo exhibition at Wembley. He did many drawings and paintings on this subject and he later wrote a book about it and held an exhibition at the Fine Art Society. Simpson exhibited regularly at the Royal Academy throughout his life and his work was frequently illustrated in 'Country Life' magazine.

The Western Union Fleet (Mounts Bay) (1949) (Penlee) is an example of Simpson's later work. Still using a light palette, this is a clever painting based on a composition of parallel lines. The line of the railing along the front is echoed by the line of people on the promenade looking at the fleet out at sea, another line is created above their heads of bunting and the line of ships on the horizon echoes this. A strong diagonal is created by the shadow across the promenade. The figures are painted in a very quick impressionist way whereas the car bonnets and headlights below the railing are painted with great detail. Simpson is using the focusing of his marks to indicate space in the painting, in much the same way as a camera lens.

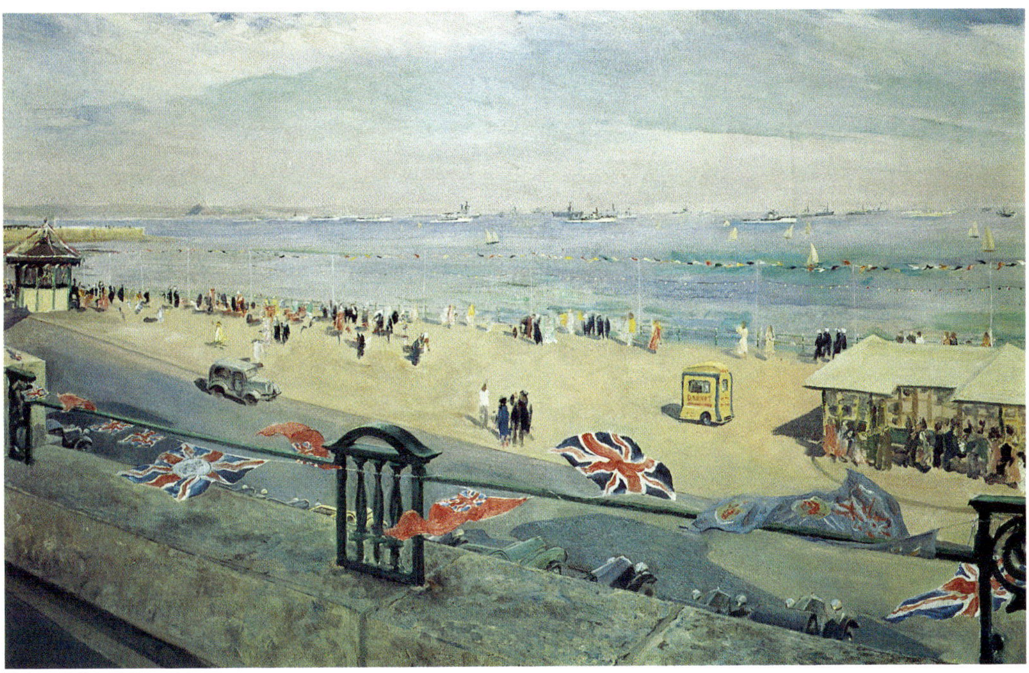

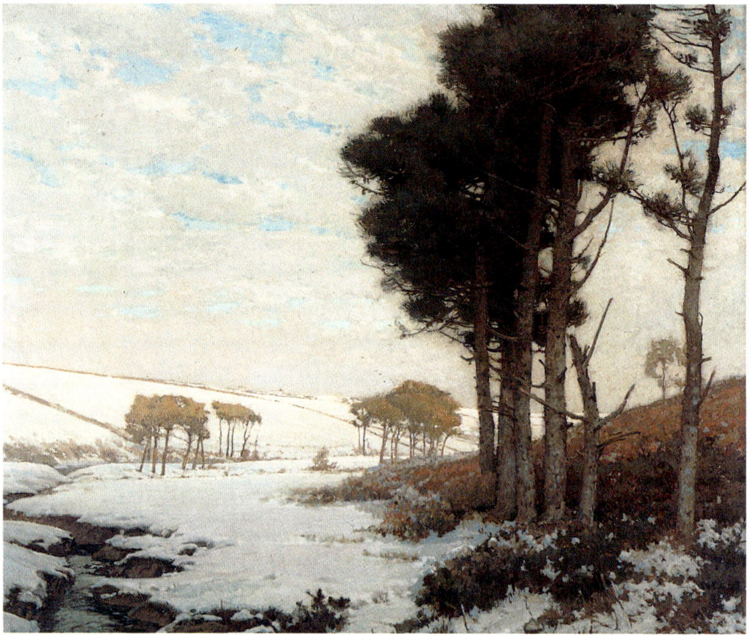

Samuel John Lamorna Birch (1869–1955) and Houghton Emily (Mouse) Birch (née Vivian) (1869–1944)

The artist who was an important focus once many students had left the Forbes' school of painting was Samuel John Birch who came to Cornwall in the early 1890s from Manchester. He had initially settled in 1892 at Boleigh Farm at the head of Lamorna Valley as opposed to coming to Newlyn. This valley is steeply wooded on either side of a stream that meets the sea at Lamorna Cove. The rocks that surround the cove are distinctive and were quarried for many years. A small harbour built up around this industry and a crane for loading boats with stone stood on the end of a short pier. This industry had all but ended by the turn of the century.

Although keen to get to know Stanhope and Elizabeth Forbes and the students at the Forbes' school, Birch has set himself apart from the Newlyners. He was first and foremost a landscape painter and recognized that Lamorna Valley was an ideal spot for painting. He made it his home and the main inspiration for his art for the rest of his working life. Birch was a self-taught artist, he learnt from practice combined with a natural-born talent, and he exhibited his first works at the age of 17. His love of landscape painting came from moving to the countryside at Halton-on-Lune in Lancashire where he would paint in his spare time from working at a mill. He had been working for the same company in Manchester in the direct production of oilcloths but the work had affected his health. In his teens he was already showing his work at Manchester City Art Gallery and selling it to patrons, such as the Storey family of Lancaster.

76
Lamorna Birch
Winter Roseworthy Valley, Camborne
c1905
oil on canvas
104.2x119.4cm
(Plymouth City Museum and Art Gallery)

77
Lamorna Birch
The Orchard
date unknown
oil on canvas
45.5x60cm
(Penlee House Gallery and Museum)

Stanhope Forbes was an important influence on the young painter and he encouraged him to go to France to study at the atelier Colarossi, which he duly did in 1895. However he spent most of his time painting on the banks of the river Seine; the resulting exhibition in Lancaster was sold out. In 1896 Birch decided to make Cornwall his permanent residence. Forbes also encouraged Birch to change his name to 'Lamorna' Birch to distinguished him from the Penzance painter Lionel Birch. Changing his name indicated how much Birch identified himself with the valley.

Birch's early style of work reflected the Victorian age and involved the use of dark colours and fine brushwork. His paintings were often of the farms and cattle in the fields. Birch was never frightened of tackling difficult weather conditions or poor lighting, in fact he seemed to revel in it and paintings of landscapes in the snow became a particular hallmark of his work at the turn of the century. *Winter Roseworthy Valley, Camborne* (c1905) (Plymouth) is a fine example of this. It was painted near where the parents of Birch's wife Houghton Emily Vivian lived. Houghton was the first private student Birch took on; she was an artist in her own right before marrying Birch in 1902 and having children. In 1902, Birch and his wife, whom he nicknamed 'Mouse', moved into Flagstaff Cottage on the top of a cliff at the sea end of the valley. Birch built his first studio in the stables of Flagstaff Cottage but later had another one built on the banks of the Lamorna stream which allowed him to combine his two great obsessions, painting and fishing. In the early days Birch used to hunt and fish in order to survive but he continued to pursue them as sports all his life. Elizabeth Forbes summed his attitude up in her ink drawing of him as the 'Painter Sportsman', which appeared in the March edition of 'Paper Chase'. Birch is shown in his hunting clothes with a shotgun under his arm.

An interesting painting, *The Orchard* (date unknown) (Penlee) is a good example of Birch's ability to be undaunted by a difficult composition. The sun is shining directly at the viewer. A modern audience will appreciate the ensuing problem when they have tried to do the

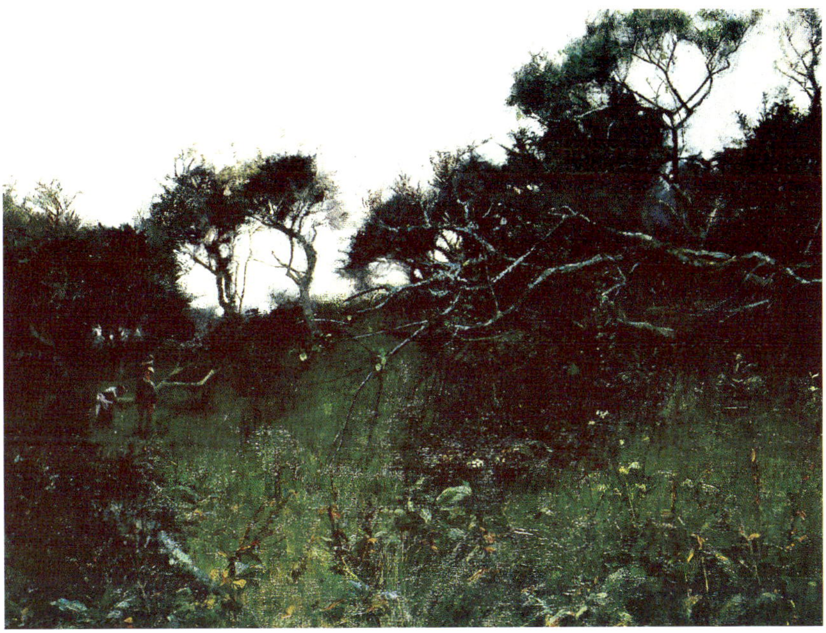

same thing with a camera. Birch solved the problem by painting the silhouetted trees on the horizon and the brightness of the sky but also filled the foreground with detailed representations of plants and undergrowth which distract the viewer from noticing the two figures in the field to the left of the scene.

Birch was always drawing and he combined his drawings with watercolours, a medium he came to excel in. He was elected a member of the Royal Society of Painters in Watercolour in 1914. His greatest achievement as a painter was his ability to depict the reflections and movement in water whether it was the sea, a loch, a river, a stream or a quarry pool. This ability was demonstrated in both watercolours and oils.

It is in his large canvases of the 1920s and 30s, which were shown every year at the Royal Academy that made Birch's name. *In Our Old World Valley* (c1921) (Penlee) was an early indication of how dramatic a painter Birch could be. It shows the stream running through Lamorna Valley to the cove beyond. This is possible as the scene is set in winter and all the trees are bare, but it is painted on a bright sunny day allowing the artist to revel in all nature's colours.

In the year he was elected an associate of the Royal Academy, Birch entered three paintings which were hung in the exhibition, one of which was *Morning Fills the Bowl* (1926) (Penlee). Birch didn't always paint exactly what he saw and this painting is a good example of how far Birch manipulated the view in order to create a powerful composition. His painting *Kerris Quarry* (1937) (Penlee) was done at the height of his powers and again shows his ability to depict reflections in water as well as create physical depth of field in his landscapes. Birch went on to paint until he was 86. His work became very commercial in the 1940s and 50s and was reproduced on thousands of greeting cards and calendars. With over 20,000 works of art to his name he was probably the most prolific of the Newlyn and Lamorna artists.

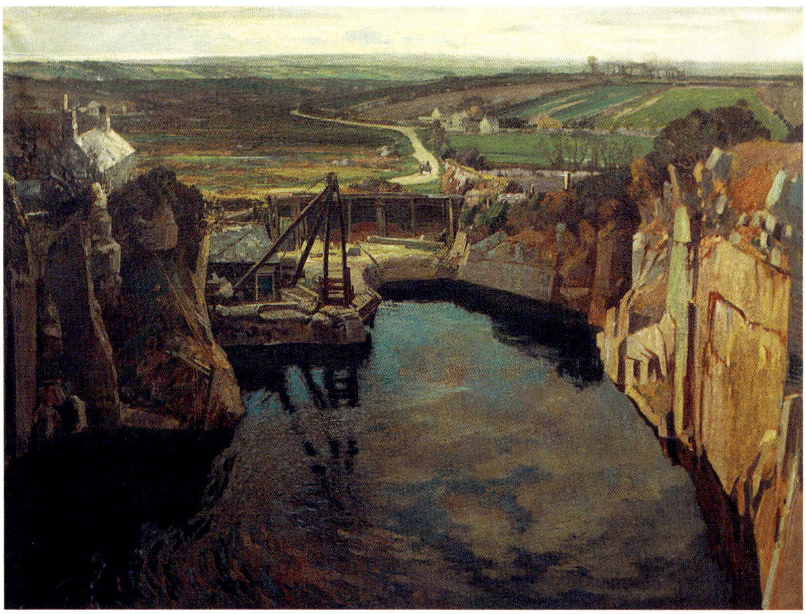

78
Lamorna Birch
Kerris Quarry 1937
oil on canvas
140x188cm
(Penlee House Gallery and Museum)

79
Lamorna Birch
In Our Old World Valley c1921
oil on canvas
100.4x125.5cm
(Penlee House Gallery and Museum)

80
John Noble Barlow *Winter Morning, Lamorna*
date unknown
oil on canvas
30.5x40.6cm
(Plymouth City Museum and Art Gallery)

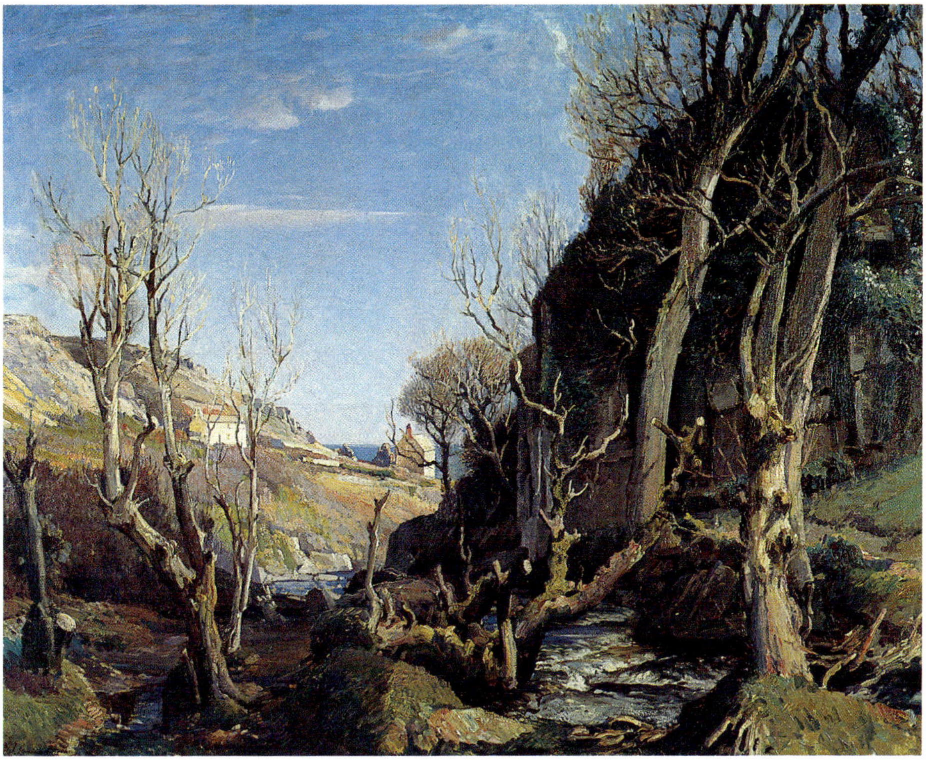

Lamorna Birch and his wife and family were the centre of social activity in Lamorna Valley and many of the artists mentioned came to live or paint in the valley to be near Birch and be part of his social and artistic circle. Like Newlyn, some artists stayed and others were only brief visitors. Some went on to attract great acclaim in the art world, others were little known outside their own circle. John Noble Barlow was an artist whose work was not dissimilar in style to Birch's, who lived in St Ives much of his working life but was a frequent visitor to Lamorna Valley and loved to paint there.

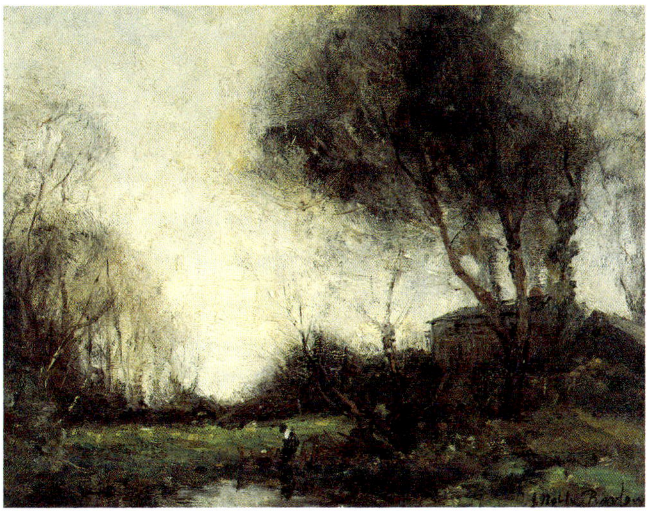

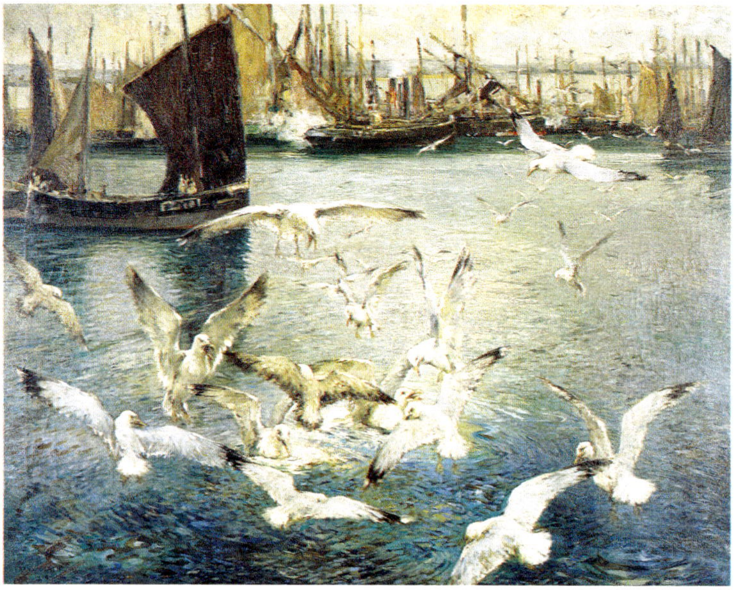

Frank Gascoigne Heath (1873–1936) and Jessica Heath (née Doherty) (1884–1967)

Frank Heath was born in Coulsdon in Surrey into a large family, being the youngest of twelve. He was the only one to show any artistic talent and went to study at the South Kensington School. He continued his studies in 1895 at the Academy of Fine Arts in Antwerp under Albrecht de Vriendt and Pierre van Hvaermaet. From 1897 to 1900 he returned to England to study at Hubert Herkomer's school at Bushey. Here Frank Heath learnt the art of etching. He had several works accepted at the Society of Oil Painters in their annual exhibition at the Piccadilly Gallery. After Bushey, Frank Heath went to Brittany to paint in the open air. The desire to paint outdoors and study under Forbes brought him to Newlyn. *Sea Birds (Gulls in Newlyn Harbour)* (1909) (Royal Cornwall Museum), which was exhibited at the Walker Gallery, Liverpool in 1909 and at the Royal Academy, reflects the Newlyn School influence as the tones of the painting are quite dark.

Jessica Doherty from Brandon in County Cork was also a student at the Forbes' school and married Frank Heath in 1910. For two years the Heaths moved to Polperro in Cornwall where they had their first children Aileen and Nancy. They returned to St Buryan where they built their house Menwinnion. Heath and his wife were great friends with the Lamorna group of artists and the influence of Birch and Laura Knight can be seen in Heath's use of much brighter bolder colours. His work in the 1920s was shown regularly at the Newlyn Art Gallery and he was coined 'the sunshine artist' by the 'Cornishman' newspaper. His subjects included interiors, seascapes and landscapes but most of them featured his family as models especially his children.

81
Frank Gascoigne Heath
Sea Birds (Gulls in Newlyn Harbour)
1909
oil on canvas
81.5x90.15cm
(Royal Cornwall Museum, Truro)

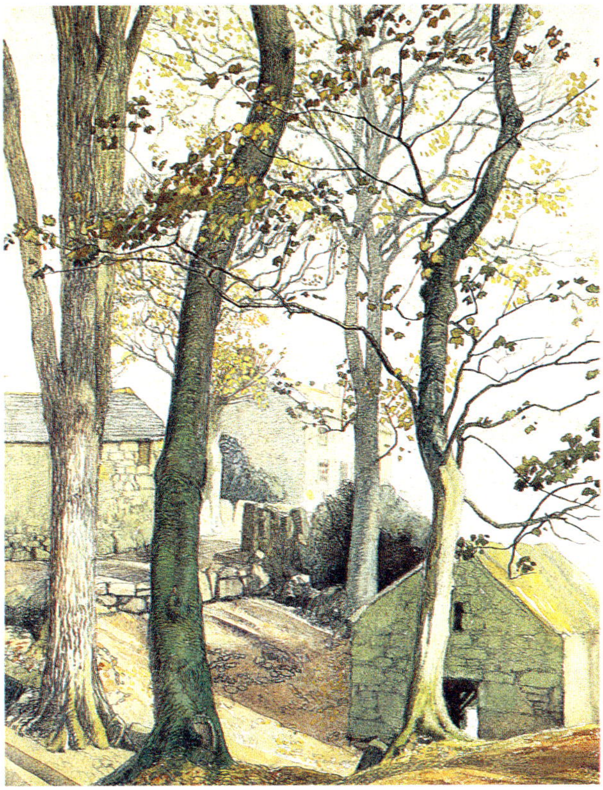

82
Eleanor Hughes
Boleigh Farm
date unknown
watercolour
48.5x39.5cm
(Penlee House Gallery and Museum)

Robert Morson Hughes (1873–1953) and Eleanor Hughes (née Waymouth) (1882–1959)

The Forbes' school not only attracted young hopefuls from around the UK, but also from abroad. Newlyn was never quite seen as the international melting pot that the St Ives colony was, but the Forbes had an international reputation by the 1900s and they were a magnet for young artists who wanted to study under them. Eleanor Waymouth came from Christchurch, New Zealand via Frank Spenlove's Yellow Door studio in London to Newlyn in 1907. Her parents were originally from the West Country. Aged 18 she won a medal for drawings of trees from the Canterbury Fine Arts Society. Her main subject was the landscape and trees in particular. Two works of Boleigh Farm by her are signed Eleanor Waymouth. These pencil drawings combined with watercolour wash show her delicate style which has been compared to that of Rennie Mackintosh. There is a huge variety of mark making in these pictures and her ability to use light and shade to create space is very accomplished. Whilst at Newlyn she met the artist Robert Hughes and married him in 1910. They settled in Lamorna and in 1912 built a house at Chyangweal near St Buryan where they lived for the rest of their lives. Eleanor Hughes was an accomplished pianist and gave recitals at her home. Later she owned her own studio in the Lamorna Valley. She and her husband travelled regularly to France and the Pyrenees. She exhibited her work at the

Royal Academy in 1911 and later at the Royal Institute of Painters in Watercolours. In 1933 she was elected a full member of the Royal Institute of Painters. She also exhibited at the New English Art Club, the Glasgow Institute, and the Walker Art Gallery, Liverpool as well as at both Newlyn and St Ives. In the last years before the War she started etching but in 1940 she sold her studio and she did little work after that date. She was a life-long friend of the Birches and the Knights; she and her husband were painted by Laura Knight.

Robert Hughes was born in Kent and studied at the Lambeth School of Art and the South London Technical College. He first came to Newlyn in 1905 where he bought one of Lamorna Birch's drawings. He returned to study at the Forbes' school of painting in 1909 where he stayed at the Cliff House Hotel. He became a great friend of Lamorna Birch as they both were interested in shooting and fishing.

Hughes was a landscape painter with a bold style as seen in his painting, *Below Carn Barges* (also known as *Rocks below Lamorna*) (date unknown) (Penlee). He captures the architectural quality of the rocks near Lamorna in this painting. He also uses the backdrop of the sea as part of the landscape with the reflection of the sun casting the rocks in shadow against it. Hughes was obviously fascinated by this juxtaposition of sea and rock as he did several other paintings on the same theme: *Tregiffian, Cornwall* (date and whereabouts unknown) and *Fog Clearing, Near St Buryan, Cornwall* (date and whereabouts unknown).

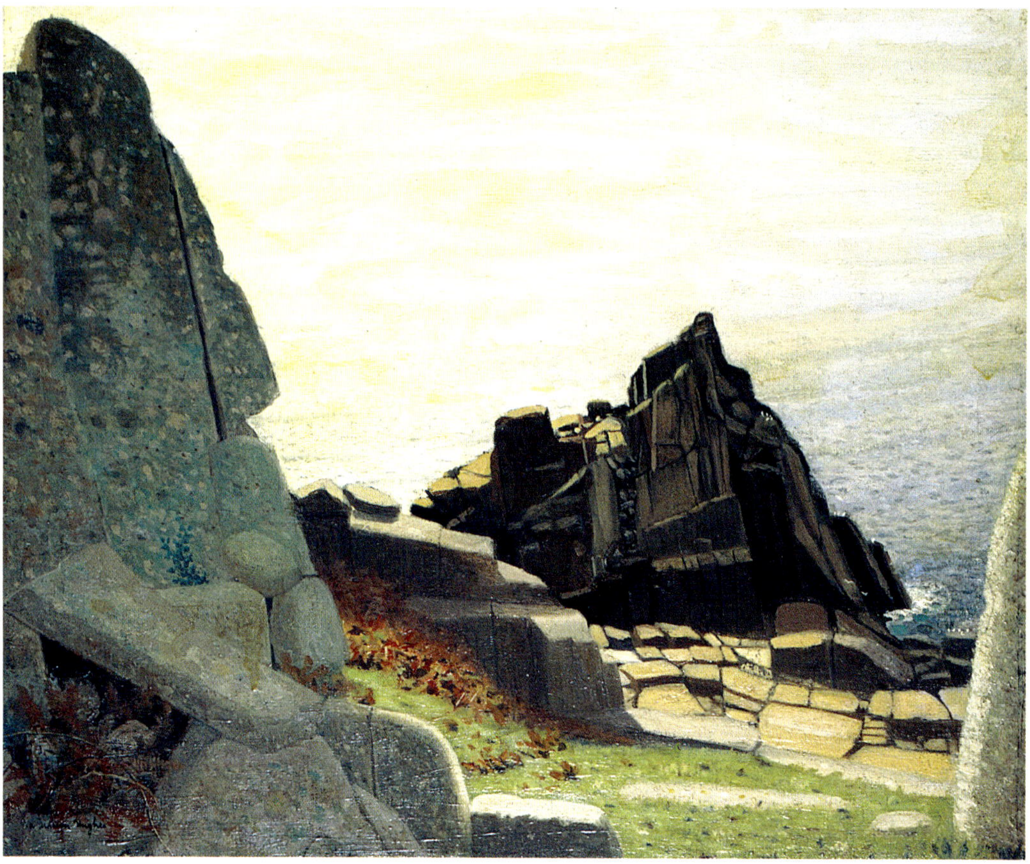

83
Robert Morson Hughes
Below Carn Barges
date unknown
oil on canvas
51.5x60.5cm
(Penlee House Gallery and Museum, on loan from Newlyn Art Gallery)

84
Stanley Gardiner
The Rickyard, Boswarthen
date unknown
oil on canvas
50.5x60.5cm
(Penlee House Gallery and Museum)

85
Marjorie Frances (Midge) Bruford
The Gypsy Camp
date unknown
oil on canvas
61.2x50.7cm
(Penlee House Gallery and Museum, on loan from Newlyn Art Gallery)

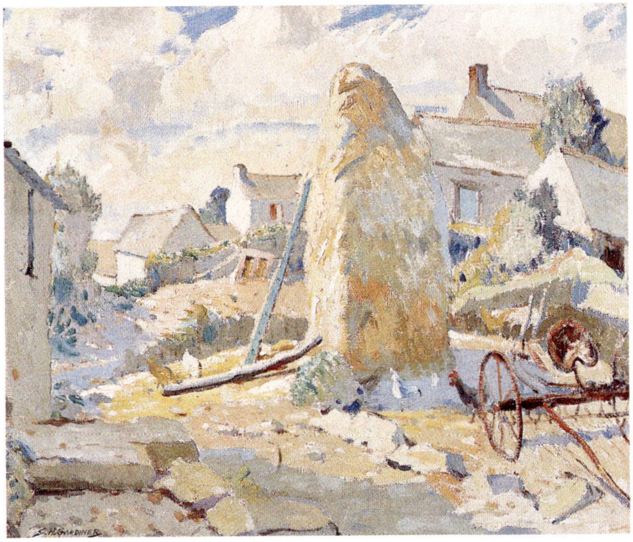

Stanley Gardiner (1887–1952) and Marjorie Frances (Midge) Bruford (1902–1958)

After meeting Birch in 1924, Stanley Gardiner came to live in Lamorna. He was born in Reading and went to evening classes in art whilst an apprentice decorator. He won a scholarship to study painting at Reading University and then went to the Allen Fraser Art College in Arbroath, Scotland. After teaching in America he returned to England in the First War and joined up. He painted landscapes and animals, especially horses and hounds. Gardiner was a great friend of Munnings and exhibited regularly at the Royal Academy between 1927 and 1947. He lived with Midge Bruford for a time in the 1930s and remained at Lily Cottage, Lamorna until his death.

The Rickyard, Boswarthen (date unknown) (Penlee) shows a similar technique to Charles Simpson using the light colours of the spectrum in an impressionist, painterly way. There is no black in this painting as he uses lilacs, oranges and blues to create shadows. *Lamorna Valley, Evening* (date unknown) (Penlee) is an atmospheric picture creating a strong sense of place, painted at the top of the valley looking down on the autumn trees.

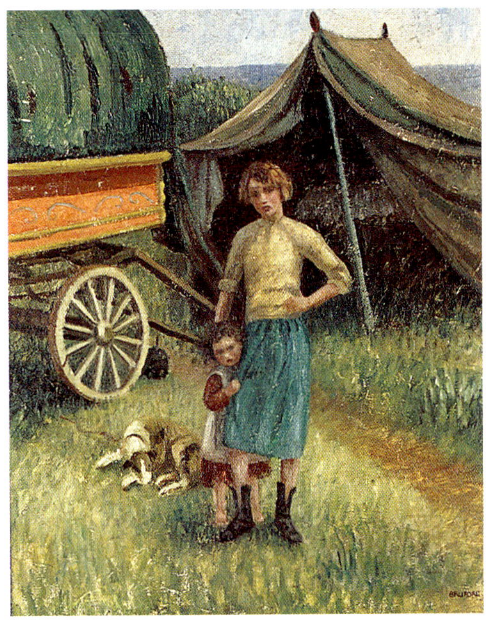

Marjorie Frances 'Midge' Bruford studied under Birch in the 1930s, having previously studied at Ernest Procter and Harold Harvey's school of painting. She modelled for Dod Procter who completed several portraits of her. She was born in Eastbourne and went to school at Badminton House, Bristol where she was friendly with Mornie Birch, Lamorna Birch's daughter. She mainly painted portraits and landscapes and signed her paintings 'Midge Bruford'. She exhibited at Newlyn Art Gallery in the 1920s as well as the Goupil Gallery, the Walker Art Gallery Liverpool, the New English Art Club and thirty-two times at the Royal Academy.

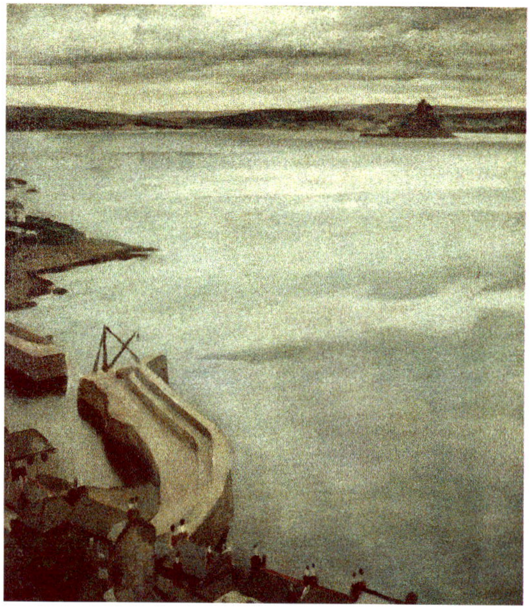

Harold Knight (1874–1961) and Laura Knight (née Johnson) (1877–1970)

Laura and Harold Knight were probably the best-known couple who came to Lamorna. They arrived in Newlyn in 1908. They were established artists, both had exhibited at the Royal Academy and held successful exhibitions at the Leicester Gallery, London in 1906 and 1907, having met whilst both were students at Nottingham School of Art. Laura was their youngest student at the time: only 13 years old. They married in 1903 and went to live in the fishing village of Staithes in Yorkshire which was another artists' colony. Laura and Harold Knight had been greatly influenced by Dutch painting which was reflected in the dark browns and blacks and dimly lit interiors in their work. But this was all to change on arrival in Cornwall.

Laura describes visiting the students at the Forbes' school in her first autobiography 'Oil Paint and Grease Paint'. She thought Dod Procter and Charles Simpson were two of the most promising students. The Knights first settled in Newlyn, initially in lodgings which were under the shadow of Paul Hill, but they soon moved to Mrs Beer's house; she was a warm and affectionate landlady who catered for their every need even offering them money when times got hard.

Laura Knight had a big studio known as Primrose Court, despite its being on top of a vegetable store and ashbin, she said it did not smell too badly. She painted outdoors making sketches for her first major paintings of Newlyn such as *The Beach*, (1908) (Laing Art Gallery) and *The Boys* (1910) (Johannesburg Art Gallery); these paintings were much lighter than her previous work. The real impetus for change came when, Benjie Leader, a painter,

86
Harold Knight
A *View of Mousehole*
date unknown
oil on canvas
49.5x44cm
(Penlee House Gallery and Museum)

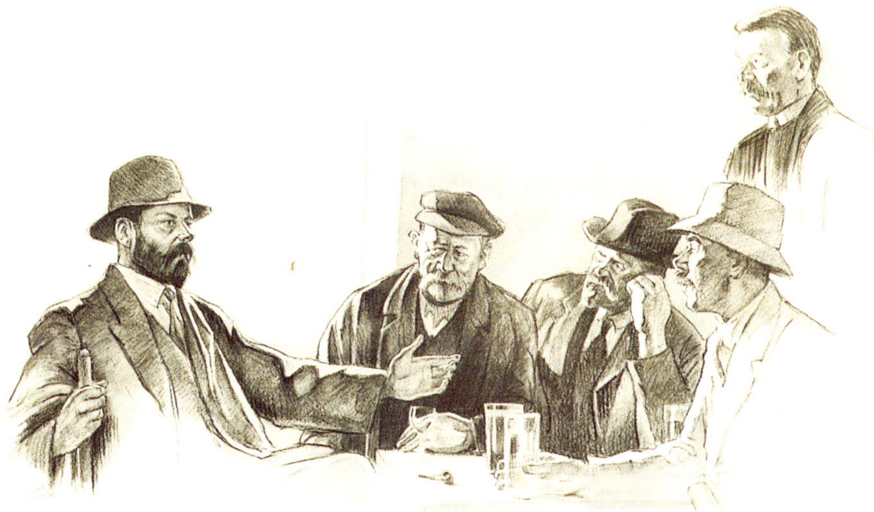

87
Harold Knight *The Council* study 1916
charcoal and wash drawing
(Royal Cornwall Museum, Truro)

lent the Knights a furnished cottage on the hill by Lamorna Gate. There Harold Knight went to paint the valley whilst Laura Knight scrambled to the rocks on the cliff edge by the sea and painted clothed and nude figures, swimming and sun bathing. She had to use models from London to pose nude for her outdoors and although locals complained, Colonel Paynter who owned the land supported Laura in her art. *Daughters of the Sun* (1911/12) (whereabouts unknown) is a good example and was well received at the Royal Academy. This was a big canvas and Laura was not put off by having to carry large canvases on her head along the coastal path several miles to her painting spot. 'I climbed along the cliff-edge and over slippery rocks every day carrying six-foot canvases on my head. It seems to me now almost a superhuman feat to have carried them so far. I was always afraid of being blown over on windy days; the canvas acted as a sail.'[38]

Harold Knight when he first came to Newlyn produced work in keeping with the Dutch influences which never really left him; A *Village Wedding* (1908) (Private Collection) was a typical Newlyn subject. A *View of Mousehole* (date unknown) (Penlee) is a muted toned grey and blue painting of a very calm sea on an overcast day. He paints this scene as if it were a still life, as if it is permanently like this. He was mainly an indoor painter and liked controlled light falling on usually well-dressed models. He did many paintings of Edith Florence Carter-Wood, who was another student at the Forbes' school and became Alfred Munnings' first wife. She was nicknamed very unattractively 'Blote', which from Harold Knight's paintings of her describes the opposite of her looks.

The Knights grew more attached to Lamorna when they moved into Trewarveneth, where the Gotches had been and later they settled in their own house at Oakhill. There was a great social life in the valley especially at Christmas. There was dancing and music and

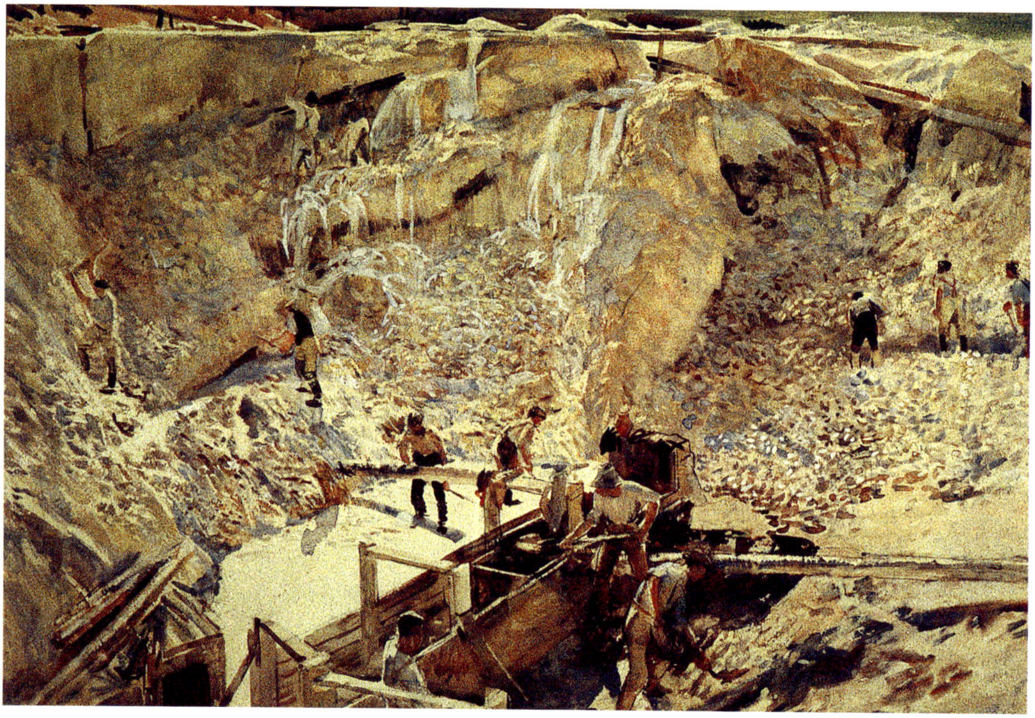

Phyllis Gotch, daughter of Thomas and Caroline, insisted on theatricals and getting everyone to dress up.

Lamorna Birch was a focal point for all the artists and Laura Knight set about painting a vast canvas of him and his two children in 1913, which she did not finish until 1934. Harold Knight's depiction of Lamorna Birch was in an interior scene set in the local pub, The Wink, where many of the artists were to be found at various times of day and night. The charcoal and wash study of the painting, called *The Council* (1916) (Royal Cornwall Museum), shows Birch on the left set apart from the others, one arm outstretched as if making an important point, Robert Hughes the painter sits opposite him. The three other figures from the left are Captain Joe Ladner, Robert Matthews, and the landlord of the pub, Old Jory, who stood in the study but is seated in the finished painting. Laura Knight was painting another large picture at this time called *Spring* (1916) (Tate Gallery). It shows the Cornish countryside in spring and a man holding his fishing rod alongside a woman with her hands on her hips. The models were good friends of the Knights: Charles and Ella Naper.

The First World War ended the carefree days of Cornwall for the Knights as getting permits to paint and draw outdoors was increasingly difficult; Harold was a conscientious objector which was not accepted at the time. He chose to work in the fields where he was left isolated for the duration of the war. This affected his health and it took him a long time to recover.

Laura Knight kept a studio in Cornwall for many years and came back to paint in the 1920s; many of her brightest, most successful depictions of women are those standing or sitting on the cliffs with the light bouncing off the sea. There is a skilfully painted watercolour by

88
Laura Knight
The China Clay Pit
1914 watercolour
45.5x69cm
(Penlee House
Gallery and
Museum)

89
Laura Knight
In the Coulisses/
Behind the Scenes
date unknown
oil on board
63x57cm
(Falmouth Art
Gallery
Collection)

Laura of *The China Clay Pit* (1914) (Penlee). It is unusual in that few Newlyn and Lamorna artists painted the industries of Cornwall, an exception being Harold Harvey.

When in London Laura found new subjects in the Diaghilev ballet and spent many hours painting the famous dancers of the day changing costume, putting on make up, rehearsing and waiting in the wings. One such picture is *In the Coulisses/Behind the Scenes* (date unknown) (Falmouth).

In the 1920s Harold Knight went to Baltimore in America to undertake portrait commissions from Dr Baer. Laura joined him and chose to paint the African Americans who were in the hospital, especially the children. The etching called *Juanita* (c1927) (Penlee) was done at this time.

Harold Knight became a successful portrait artist and was elected a Royal Academician in 1937, the same year he was made president of the Nottingham Society of Artists. Harold Knight never achieved the same renown as his wife Laura, as he was a much quieter person, who painted modest pictures, but he was a very accomplished and skilful painter. Laura Knight went on to be made a Dame for her achievements and was elected to the Royal Academy in 1935.

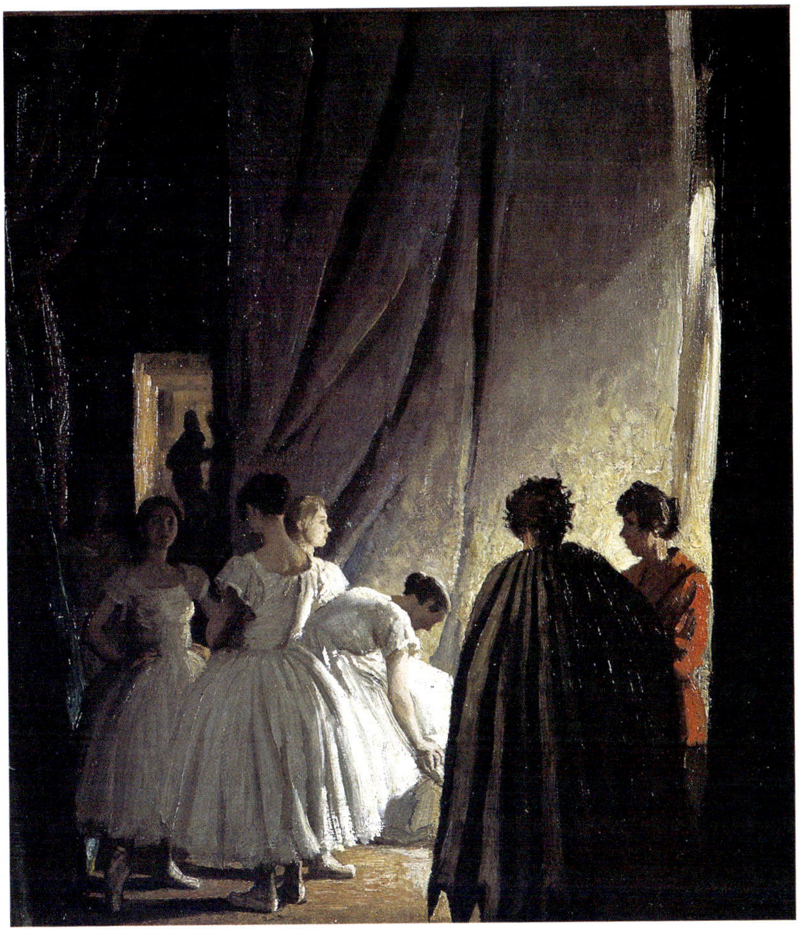

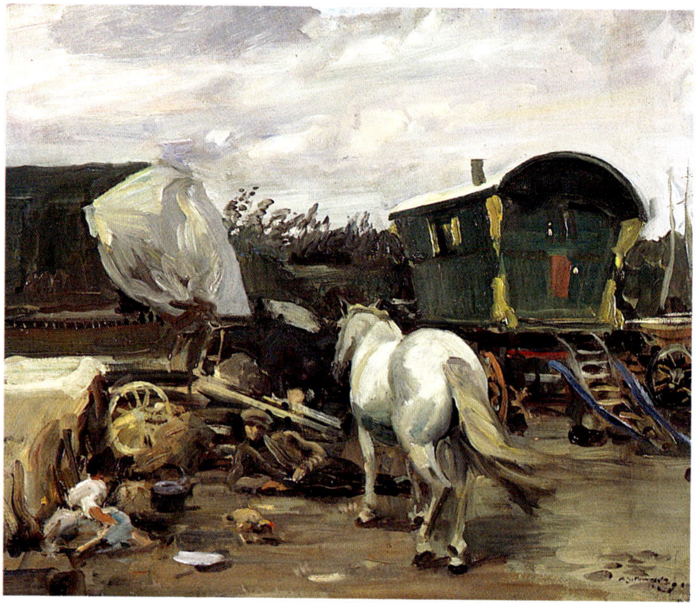

90
Alfred
Munnings
The Caravan
date unknown
oil on canvas
50x60cm
(Falmouth Art
Gallery
Collection)

Alfred Munnings (1878–1959)

Laura Knight greatly admired Alfred Munnings who came to Cornwall in 1908. He had a big impact on the Newlyn and Lamorna artists both in terms of his painting and his personality. He lived at Chywoone Farm when he first came to Newlyn, and later moved to Lamorna where he had rooms at the Wink; his studio was in an old mill. Surrounded by female admirers, he took charge of the social life, organizing musical evenings that could often get out of control. He used Cornwall as a backdrop in his paintings for his depictions of horses and hounds.

Using Lamorna as a base, Munnings travelled to Binstead, near Alton in Hampshire to paint the gypsy hop-pickers. In *The Caravan* (c 1913) (Falmouth) we see the gypsies lying around their camp fire. Munnings describes a similar scene in his autobiography 'An Artist's Life': 'Lurchers and greyhounds lay underneath many a vehicle, travelling families of fowls were making themselves at home around the fences and smoke from wood fires, shouts of fighting children and barking dogs filled the air.' [39]

He also loved the coast and spent several weeks painting in Zennor. Munnings met Edith Florence Carter-Wood who was visiting her brother, Joey, a student at the Forbes' school. In *The Morning Ride* (c1912) (Private Collection) Munnings painted her sitting on a horse in the dappled sunlight. Other than horses and art they had little in common and their marriage in 1912 was doomed, ending two years later when Florence committed suicide by taking cyanide. Munnings became an important portrait and animal painter to the English aristocracy after the First World War; he settled in Dedham, Norfolk where he married Violet McBride. He became a Royal Academician in 1926 and was elected President of the Royal Academy and was particularly famous for his resigning speech debunking modern art.

91
Photo of Ella Naper (Private Collection)

92
Ella Naper
left: *Pendant* (ballet dancer in enamel by Laura Knight into a setting by Ella Naper marked 'EN & LK 1916')
right: *Silver, Enamel Moonstone and Mother of Pearl Necklace with Matching Earrings*
date unknown
(Private Collection)

93
Ella Naper
Egyptian Dancers
date unknown
enamel on copper 4x5cm
(Private Collection)

94
Ella Naper
Ballerina (green and white)
1914/15
enamel on copper 4x5cm
signed LK &EN
(Private Collection)

95
Ella Naper
Ballerina (gold and blue)
1914/15
enamel on copper 4x5cm
signed LK &EN
(Private Collection)

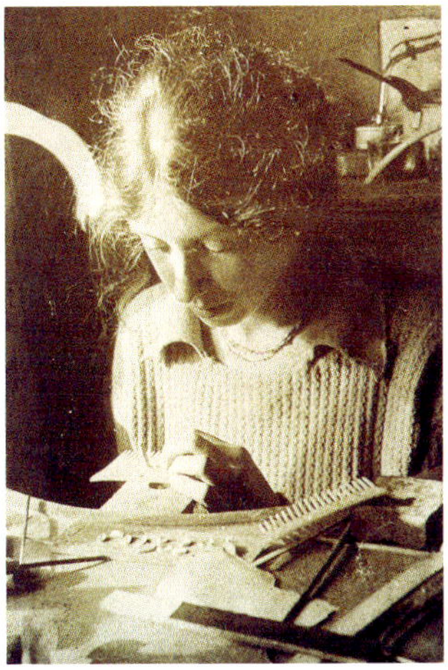

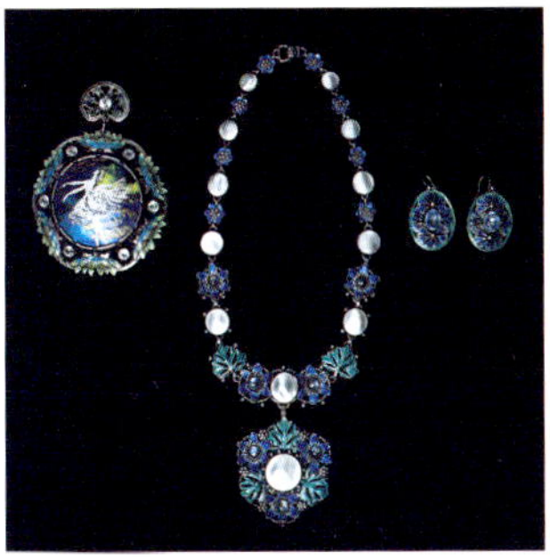

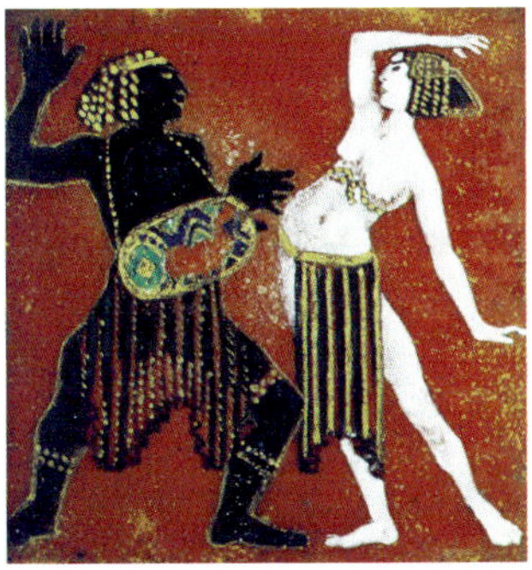

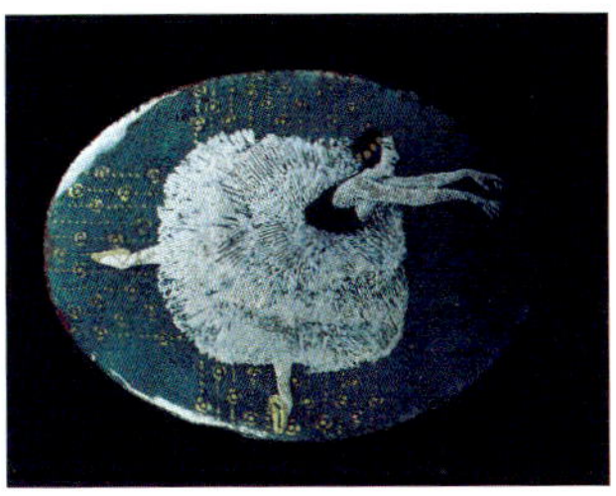

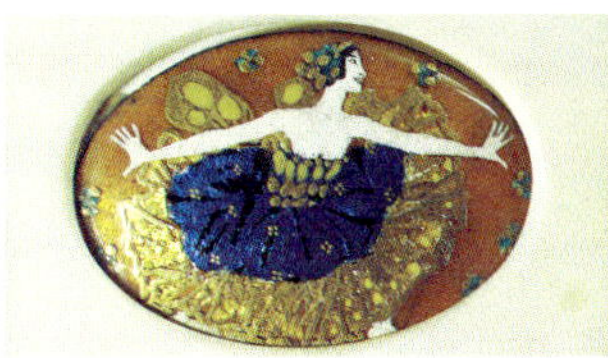

Charles Naper (1882–1968) and Ella Naper (née Champion) (1886–1972)

Charles Naper was born in Devon and had studied architecture for a short time before going to the Royal Academy School. When he returned to Devon he met and fell in love with Ella Champion, a gifted jewellery maker and painter. They moved to Lamorna and built their own house, Trewoofe, after a short stay in Looe, East Cornwall. Trewoofe was to remain their family home. Charles did many studies of the cliffs and landscapes around Land's End. Sadly little of his work exists as the criticism he received when he did exhibit it made him destroy most of it.

Ella Naper was born in New Cross in London and went to Camberwell School of Arts and Crafts studying jewellery under Fred Partridge. In 1906 she joined a workshop group of jewellers set up by Partridge in Branscombe in South Devon. Ella Naper's jewellery ranged from delicate necklaces, earrings and brooches made from silver with stone settings to organically shaped combs and hair slides based on plants, flowers and insects in the tradition of Art Nouveau design. She sold her work locally and in London at Liberty's and at the Women's Art Exhibition. Ella Naper collaborated with Laura Knight on several small enamels, which were based on ballet dancers Laura Knight had seen at Diaghilev's ballet in London. Ella Naper was also a life model for Laura Knight on many occasions. She describes Ella Naper in her autobiography as 'an adorably lovely slim creature, brown as a berry'.[40] She was also an accomplished watercolourist and the skill and observation of flowers and plants in her paintings obviously influenced the precision and accuracy of her jewellery making. She exhibited at the Walker Art Gallery, Liverpool twenty one times as well as in London at the Royal Society of British Artists and the International Society. She carried out many public commissions including mayoral chains and plaques including a plaque for Exeter Cathedral made in pewter and enamel and another for Charles Church, Plymouth.

The Napers, the Knights and the Harveys all used to go up to Dozmary Pool on Bodmin Moor, where the Napers had a small painting hut. The artists would picnic and paint and swim and get away from the hectic whirl of the Newlyn scene.

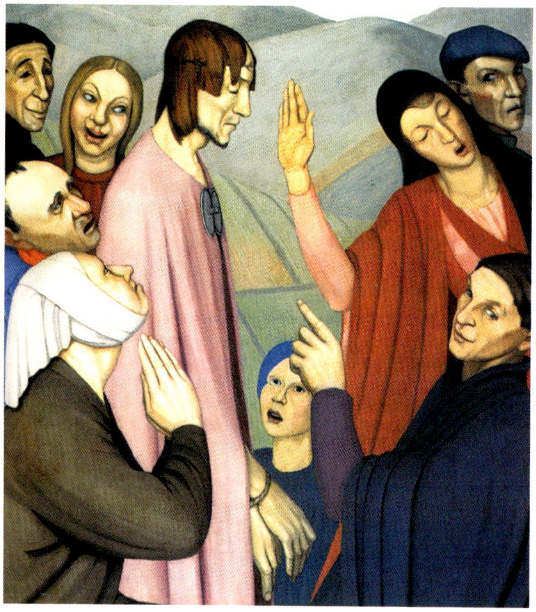

Anne Walke (née Fearon) (1888–1965)

An important figure in the Newlyn and Lamorna community was the Reverend Bernard Walke, who Laura Knight captured beautifully in a charcoal portrait. He was a Catholic Anglican, brought up in the Catholic tradition and was part of a movement in the Church of England to bring the latter closer to the Church of Rome. He became well known for his Cornish plays produced for Christmas and Easter and All Soul's Eve, which were performed by the congregation in the style of the old miracle plays. In 1926, his play 'Bethlehem' was broadcast from St Hilary Church by the BBC; this was repeated for many years. Father Walke also set about renovating St Hilary Church. Although initially shy of meeting the Lamorna artists, through Alfred Munnings who was a friend of his wife's, he got to know the Knights, the Harveys and the Procters who all became involved with Anne Walke and her old art college friend Gladys Hynes in decorating the church by depicting the Cornish saints on bright colourful panels.

Anne Walke, his artist wife, was born in London and studied at Chelsea School of Art and at the London School of Art where amongst her tutors were Sir William Nicholson (1872–1949) and Augustus John (1878–1961). She first came to Cornwall with her husband when he was a curate in Polruan. It seemed an odd coupling but as a shopkeeper replied to Anne's sister, Hilda Fearon, on complaining her sister was going to marry a curate, 'If a curate can put up with an artist, surely an artist can put up with a curate.'[41] In 1912 they moved to St Hilary where Bernard Walke became vicar; Anne Walke continued to paint. One of her most impressive portraits is of her husband and his mother. The colours in this painting are quite dark and conventional.

96
Anne Walke
Christ Mocked
c1935
oil on canvas
(Royal Cornwall Museum, Truro)

97
Anne Walke
Rev Bernard Walke and his Mother
date unknown
oil on canvas
(Royal Cornwall Museum, Truro)

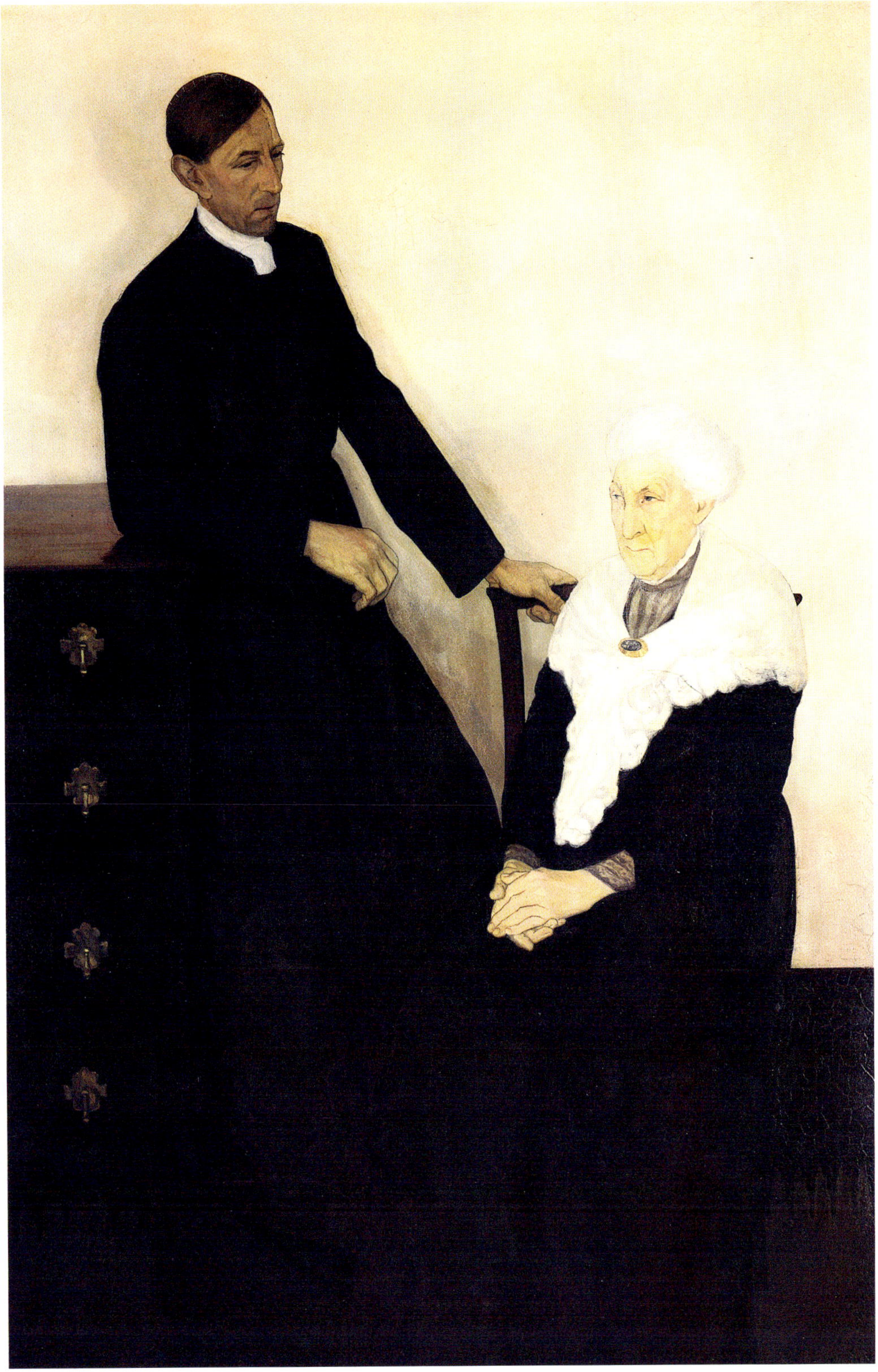

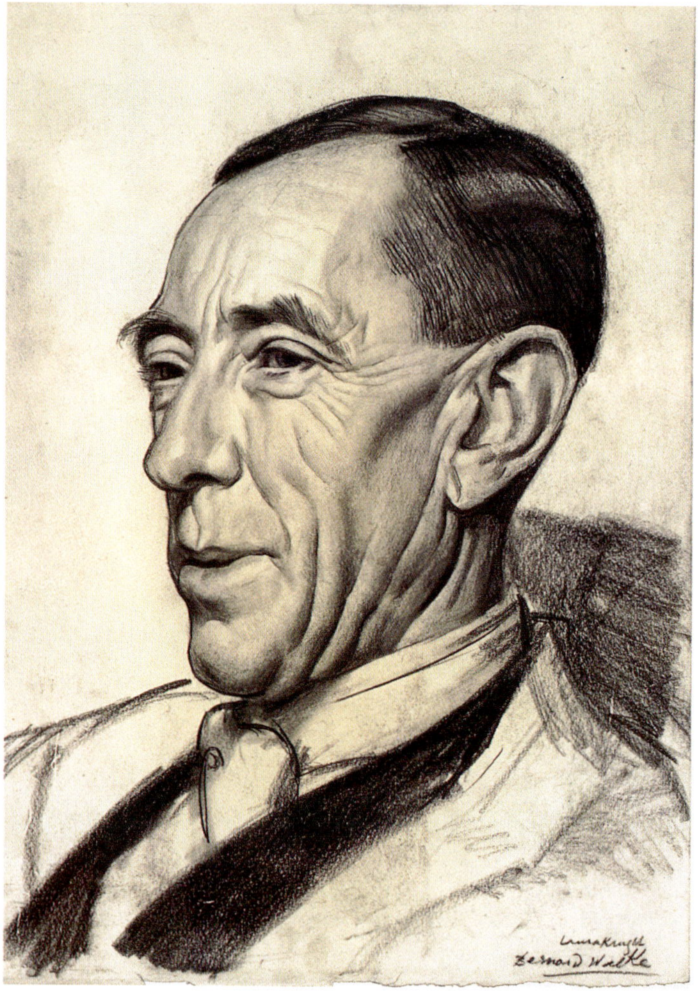

It was in her religious works that her colour came to life. *Preaching from the Hill* (date unknown) (Royal Cornwall Museum) and *Christ Mocked* (c1935) (Royal Cornwall Museum) are two good examples of Anne's biblical painting. They are set against rolling green countryside, probably inspired by the hills of West Penwith. The figures are highly stylized but painted wearing richly coloured clothes. Anne carried out many commissions for churches including the altarpiece triptych for Truro Cathedral as well for her husband's church at St Hilary. She exhibited her work in London at the Goupil Gallery, the Leicester Gallery, the Royal Academy, the Royal Institute of Oil Painters and the Society of Women Artists.

98
Laura Knight
Portrait of Bernard Walke
date unknown
charcoal on paper 38x27cm
(Penlee House Museum and Gallery)

99
Stanhope Forbes
Village Rendezvous, Copperhouse Creek
1938
oil on canvas, 78x62.5cm
(Plymouth City Museum and Art Gallery)

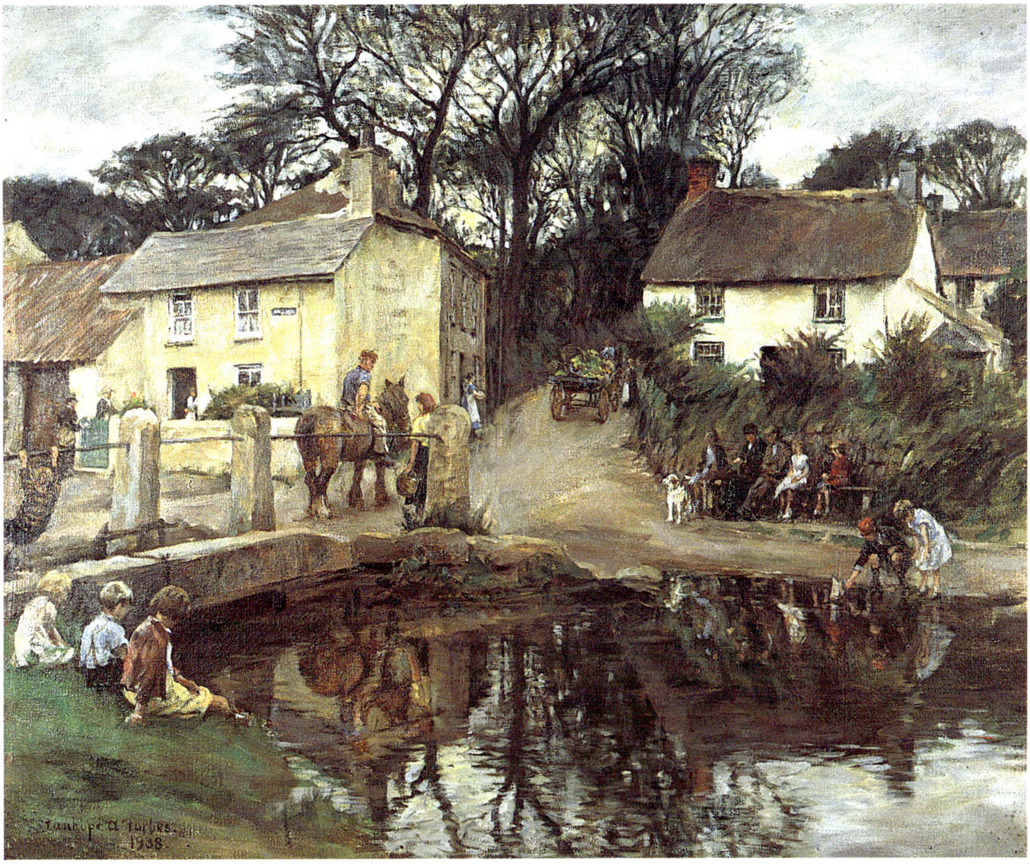

The End of an Era

Stanhope Forbes continued to teach at the Forbes' school of painting up until the Second World War. After the death of Elizabeth in 1912, he married Maudie Palmer in 1915 who was an artist and had been a pupil; she continued to work with Forbes at the school. Stanhope Forbes was affectionately known as the 'Professor' and he provided the link between the old Newlyn School and the next generation. He continued to paint in the 1920s and 30s mainly landscapes including *Relubbus Bridge* (1929) (Penlee) and *Village Rendezvous, Copperhouse Creek* (1938) (Plymouth). He also depicted several townscapes in the 1930s of Penzance, Helston and Penryn. These paintings are first and foremost topographical and the architecture of the streets dominates the painting, with cars, people and horses and carts as secondary elements. Forbes was one of the artists, as was Lamorna Birch, commissioned by the Great Western Railway to design railway posters.

There are those who think that Forbes' paintings went decidedly downhill hill after 1912 becoming 'repeatedly repetitious and at times slick.'[42] It is true that Forbes by the 1920s and 30s had been left behind by the rapid changes in artistic practice elsewhere, as were many of the artists of the Newlyn and Lamorna colonies. The rise of Modernism and abstraction brought the era of *plein air* painting to an end as a leading art form. The First World War had not deterred artists from coming to Cornwall, although there were restrictions on painting and drawing outdoors. By the Second World War things had changed and Forbes' death in 1947 marked the end of an era for painting in the Newlyn and Lamorna art colonies; the focus for art in Cornwall shifted to the modernists in St Ives.

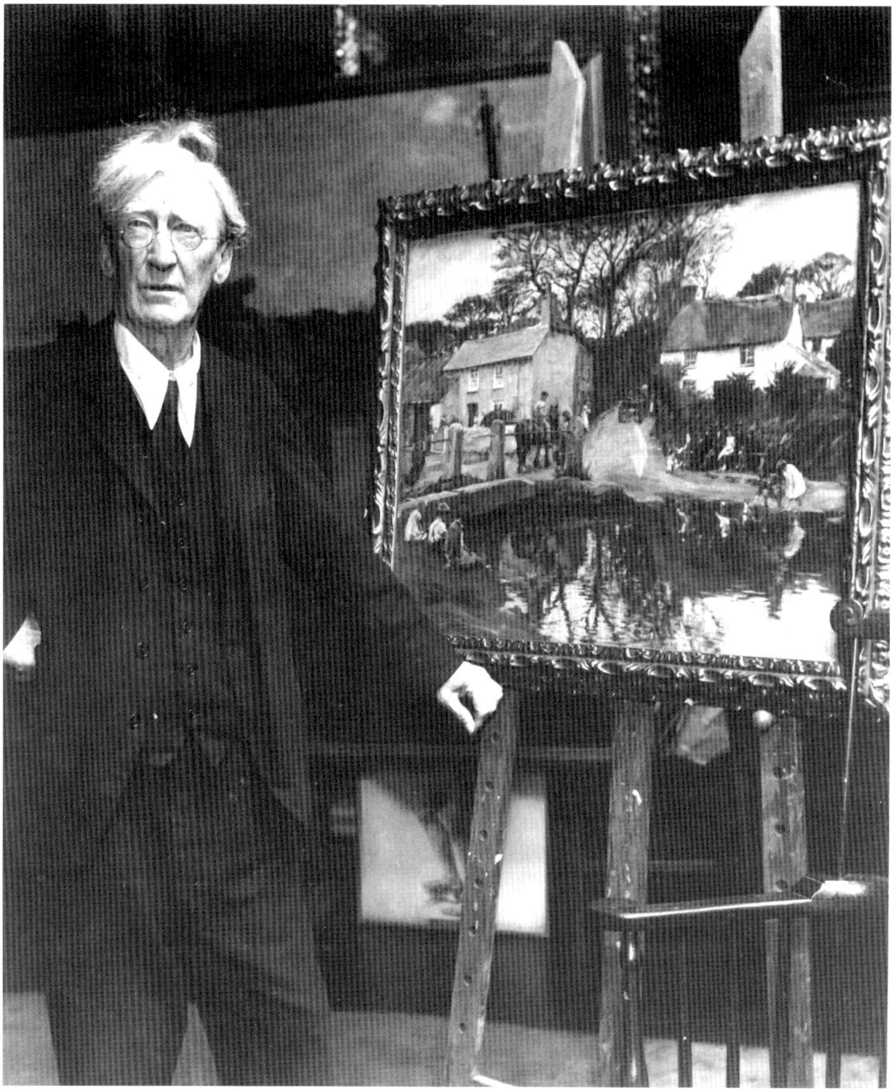

100
Photo of
Stanhope Forbes
c 1938 with
Village Rendezvous, Copperhouse Creek
(West Cornwall Art Archive)

Afterword

Where do the Newlyn and Lamorna art colonies fit not only into British but global art history? What was their contribution? Is it just work about a certain time and place? Were the artists any good?

These are all questions you may have asked yourself when you first picked up this book. I hope I have given you enough information to make up your own mind as art history is always a matter of opinion.

The Newlyn and Lamorna artists produced a body of work which started out being fairly radical as it brought, not necessarily new but, unfamiliar techniques from the continent to a British audience. This was not unique as other artists were returning from the continent to their home countries with similar ideas.

The fact that this particular group of artists chose this particular place and people to depict did make the work identifiable in a special way. What Stanhope and Elizabeth Forbes and their followers contributed certainly to the British art scene was exporting the good practice of art teaching from the urban heartland into a rural setting, proving that high standards could be maintained and that good work could be made outside London. These were not 'holiday painters' who might come to paint Cornwall just because they knew it would give them pretty pictures. These were serious artists who were making their reputation on the work they produced in Cornwall.

In the 1880s the Newlyn painters who were Social Realists made comments about poverty which was, and still is, a universal subject. With the influence of the bright colours of the continent at the beginning of the 20th century, the depictions of Cornwall became much lighter and on the whole advertised well-being and a good life. Indeed, the artists' colonies of Newlyn and Lamorna along with that of St Ives produced some of the first images promoting Cornwall as a holiday destination to the outside world. By the 1920s and 30s the paintings being created were no longer seen as ground-breaking, in fact they were part of a tradition which the colony itself had created and when art starts to be mainly concerned with references to itself, it becomes stultified and dead.

During the 1940s and 50s when Modernism ruled it was very hard for many of the Newlyn and Lamorna artists to make a living and they realised that fashions had changed and that art in Newlyn and Lamorna had to change. But the pendulum of fashion swings back and forth and so, as the resurgence of interest in the Newlyn School in the last 20 years demonstrates, there is still an audience for representational works of the figure and landscape. Maybe this is based on pure nostalgia as the Newlyn and Lamorna painters captured an idyllic world. However, the greatest test of any artist's work is time, and certainly the strength of any group of artists relies upon the strength of individuals within it. Therefore, although not every artist who came to Newlyn and Lamorna was a master, they all had something to offer and by working in close proximity to each other, a genre of work was created which had a power greater than the sum of its parts.

Notes

1 'A lady reviewer' of the 1888 RA exhibition quoted by Wilfred Meynell in 1905 in the Windsor Magazine
2 Caroline Fox *Stanhope Forbes and the Newlyn School* p13
3 Maria Tuke Sainsbury *Henry Scott Tuke*
4 Michael Jacobs *The Good and Simple Life* p44
5 Mr Edwin Harris *Edgbastonia Vol* XIX July 1899 p124
6 Judith Cook, Melissa Hardie and Christiana Payne *Singing from the Walls, the life and art of Elizabeth Armstrong Forbes* p49
7 K Harris *Hevva! Cornish Fishing in the Days of Sail* p33
8 K Harris *Hveva! Cornish Fishing in the Days of Sail* p33
9 A Perambulating Contributor to *The Cornishman* newspaper
10 Letter to Forbes' mother autumn 1885
11 Letter to Forbes' mother April18th 1886
12 Caroline Fox *Stanhope Forbes and the Newlyn School* p24
13 Letter from Bellevue April 1884
14 Mrs Lionel Birch *Stanhope Forbes and Mrs Elizabeth Stanhope Forbes* p30
15 Alice Meynell 'Newlyn' in *The Art Journal* April 1889 p101
16 Alice Meynell 'Newlyn' in *The Art Journal* April 1889 p101–102
17 Letter May 31st 1885
18 Mrs Lionel Birch *Stanhope Forbes and Mrs Elizabeth Stanhope Forbes* p97
19 Letter to Forbes' mother February 1st 1888
20 Frank Bramley catalogue Usher Galley, Lincoln 1999 p29
21 Letter to Forbes' mother February 1885
22 Letter to Forbes' mother October 198h 1888
23 Letter to Forbes' mother November 19th 1885
24 Review referring to A *Minuet* quoted Cook, Hardie and Payne *Singing from the Walls* p94
25 *The Cornishman* April 5th 1894
26 Betsy Cogger Rezelman *The Newlyn Artists and their Place in Victorian Art* Phd 1984 West Cornwall Art Archive
27 Gladys Beattie Crozier *Every Woman's Encyclopædia*, 'The Newlyn Art School' p282
28 Gladys Beattie Crozier *The Girl's Realm*, 'The Newlyn School of Painting, Mr and Mrs Forbes as Teachers' Nov. 1904 p109
29 Mrs Lionel Birch *Stanhope Forbes and Mrs Elizabeth Stanhope Forbes* p110
30 Mrs Lionel Birch *Stanhope Forbes and Mrs Elizabeth Stanhope Forbes* p116
31 *Paper Chase* 1909
32 Laura Knight *Oil Paint and Grease Paint* p161/62
33 *Colour* April 1919.
34 Malcolm Pilcher a professional engraver quoted in *The Cornishman* 14 May 1988 by Frank Ruhrmund
35 Hazel Berriman *Arts and Crafts in Newlyn* 1890–1930
36 Letter to Ruth Alison's mother, quoted in A *Breath of Fresh Air* by John Branfield p 82
37 Prospectus of the St Ives School of Painting 1916
38 Laura Knight *Oil Paint and Grease Paint* p175/76
39 Alfred Munnings *An Artist's Life* p105
40 Laura Knight *Oil Paint and Grease Paint* p201
41 Bernard Walke *Twenty Years at St Hilary* p 87
42 Caroline Fox *Stanhope Forbes and the Newlyn School*

Further Reading

Bedford, Hugh, *Frank Gascoigne Heath* H. Bedford 1995

Bendiner, Kenneth, *An Introduction to Victorian Painting*, Yale University Press New Haven and London 1985

Berriman, Hazel, *Arts and Crafts in Newlyn* 1890–1930, Newlyn Orion 1986

Berriman, Hazel, *Cryséde, the unique textile designs of Alec Walker*, The Royal Institution of Cornwall 1993

Birch, Mrs Lionel, *Stanhope Forbes and Mrs Elizabeth Stanhope Forbes*, Cassell and Co 1906

Cook, Judith, Hardie, Melissa, and Payne, Christiana, *Singing from the Walls, The Life and Art of Elizabeth Forbes* Sansom & Co in association with Penlee House Gallery & Museum, Penzance 2000

Cross, Tom, *The Shining Sands, Artists in Newlyn and St Ives*, 1880–1930, Halsgrove 1994

Fox, Caroline, *Dame Laura Knight*, Phaidon Press 1988

Fox, Caroline, *Stanhope Forbes and the Newlyn School*, David and Charles 1993

Hardie, Melissa, 100 *Years in Newlyn, Diary of a Gallery*, Patten Press 1985

Jacobs, Michael, *The Good and Simple Life – Artist Colonies in Europe and America*, Phaidon 1985.

Knight, Laura, *Oil Paint and Grease Paint*, Nicholson and Watson 1936

Langley, Roger, *Walter Langley, – Pioneer of the Newlyn Art Colony*, Sansom & Company in association with Penlee House Gallery & Museum, Penzance, 1997.

McConkey, Kenneth, Risdon, Peter and Sheppard, Pauline, *Harold Harvey, Painter of Cornwall*, Sansom & Co. in association with Penlee House Gallery & Museum, Penzance 2001

Postle, Martin, and Vaughan, William, *The Artists Model from Etty to Spencer*, Merrrell Holberton 1999

Sainsbury, Maria Tuke, *Henry Scott Tuke*, Secker 1933

Wainwright, David, and Dinn, Catherine, *Under Canvas, Henry Scott Tuke* (1858–1929), Sarema Press 1989

Walke, Bernard, *Twenty Years at St Hilary* new edition Truran 2002

Wormleighton, Austin, A *Painter Laureate Lamorna Birch and his Circle*, Sansom and Co 1995

Exhibition Catalogues

Canney, Michael, *Norman and Alethea Garstin* 1978

Fox, Caroline, and Greenacre, Francis, *Artists of the Newlyn School* (1880–1900), Newlyn Orion 1979

Fox, Caroline, and Greenacre, Francis, *Painting in Newlyn and Lamorna* 1880–1930, The Barbican Art Gallery and Newlyn Orion 1985

Greg, Andrew, *Charles Napier Hemy* (1841–1917) Tyne and Wear County Council Museums 1984

Hardie, Melissa, Whybrow, Marion, and Reardon, Valerie, *Women Artists in Cornwall* 1880–1940, essays by, complied by Catherine Wallace, Falmouth Town Council 1996

Holmes, Jonathan, *An Artistic Tradition, Two Centuries of Painting and Craft in West Cornwall*, 1750–1950, Penlee House Gallery and Museum 1993

Lincolnshire County Council, *Frank Bramley* RA 1857–1915 1999

Newlyn Orion *Painting in Newlyn* (1900–1930) 1985

Laing Art Gallery and Newlyn Orion Gallery, *Dod Procter* RA 1892–1972 1990

Paintings Illustrated from the Galleries of Cornwall and Plymouth

Falmouth Art Gallery, Municipal Buildings, The Moor, Falmouth TR11 2RT
Tel: 01326 313863 www.falmouthartgallery.com

38 Hemy Charles Napier *Haul Aft!*
37 Hemy Charles Napier *Falmouth Town*
89 Knight Laura *Behind the Scenes/In the Coulisses*
90 Munnings Alfred *The Caravan*
42 Tuke Henry Scott *Boys Bathing* study
41 Tuke Henry Scott *French Barque in Falmouth*
43 Tuke Henry Scott *The Message*
40 Tuke Henry Scott *St Tropez*

Penlee House Museum and Gallery, Morrab Road, Penzance TR18 4HE
Tel: 01736 363625 www.penleehouse.org.uk

79 Birch Lamorna *In Our Old World Valley*
78 Birch Lamorna *Kerris Quarry*
77 Birch Lamorna *The Orchard*
85 Bruford Midge *The Gypsy Camp*
34 Craft Percy *Hevva! Hevva!*
35 Craft Percy *Tucking a School of Pilchards on the Cornish Coast*
10 Evans Frederick James McNamara *Old Fisherman*
52 Fletcher William Teulon Blandford *Bosham Harbour at Low Tide*
45 Forbes Elizabeth *A Minuet*
46 Forbes Elizabeth *A Newlyn Maid*
8 Forbes Elizabeth *A Zandvoort Fisher Girl*
6 Forbes Elizabeth *Boy with a Stick*
7 Forbes Elizabeth *Peeling Onions*
44 Forbes Elizabeth *School is Out*
61 Forbes Stanhope *The Young Apprentice, Newlyn Copperworks*
22 Forbes Stanhope *The Violinist (Walter Barnes)*
9 Fortescue William Banks *Newlyn Old Harbour*
84 Gardiner Stanley *The Rickyard, Boswarthen*
71 Garnier Geoffrey *Lamorna Cove*
56 Garstin Norman *The Rain it Raineth Everyday*
29 Gotch Thomas Cooper *Girl in a Cornish Garden*
49 Hall Fred *In the Fields*
19 Harris Edwin *Old Fisherwoman*
18 Harris Edwin *The Lesson*
61 Harvey Harold *Girl on a Cliff*
82 Hughes Eleanor *Boleigh Farm*
83 Hughes Robert *Below Carn Barges*
86 Knight Harold *A View of Mousehole*
88 Knight Laura *The China Clay Pit*
98 Knight Laura *Bernard Walke*
13 Langley Walter *Among the Missing (Scene in a Cornish Fishing Village)*
12 Langley Walter *Breadwinners*
15 Langley Walter *In a Cornish Fishing Village; the Departure of the Fleet to the North*
17 Langley Walter *The Sunny South*
53 Millard Fred *The Thread Runs Smooth as Yet*
60 Newlyn Copper

68 Procter Ernest *Porthgwarra*
69 Procter Dod *Portrait of Eileen Mayo*
70 Procter Dod *Aunt Lilla*
75 Simpson Charles *The Western Union Fleet, Mounts Bay*
74 Simpson Ruth *Maroon and Gold*
51 Tayler Alexander Chevallier *Shelling Peas*
33 Todd Ralph *Primrose Day*
67 Walker Alec Cryséde design *Cherry Tree*
66 Walker Alec *Men Working in the Violet Fields, Trembath*

Plymouth City Museum and Art Gallery, Drake Circus, Plymouth PL4 8AJ
Tel: 01752 304774 www.plymouth.gov.uk

80 Barlow Noble *Winter Morning, Lamorna*
76 Birch Lamorna *Winter, Roseworthy Valley*
21 Forbes Stanhope *Old Martin Sampson*
20 Forbes Stanhope *Fish Sale on a Cornish Beach*
99 Forbes Stanhope *Village Rendezvous, Copperhouse Creek*
1 Garstin Norman *Among the Pots*
4 Garstin Norman *Church of St Michèle, Quimperlé*
63 Harvey Harold *Newlyn Harbour*
62 Harvey Harold *Sport on Shore*
36 Hemy Charles Napier *A Shrimper's Daughter*
59 Hunter Sherwood *A Place of Wailing*
16 Langley Walter *When One is Old*
39 Tuke Henry Scott *Taking a Spell*
73 Simpson Charles *Line Fishing, St. Ives*

Royal Cornwall Museum, River Street, Truro TR1 2SJ
Tel: 01872 272205 www.royalcornwallmuseum.org.uk

31 Bramley Frank *The Truce*
47 Forbes Elizabeth *Woodland Scene: As You Like It*
25 Forbes Stanhope *Against Regatta Day*
23 Forbes Stanhope *The Lighting Up Time* study
24 Forbes Stanhope *The Seine Boat* study
55 Garstin Norman *Her Signal*
26 Gotch Thomas Cooper *Sharing Fish*
50 Hall Fred *Josiah Wright*
64 Harvey Harold *St Just Tin Miners*
81 Heath Frank Gascoigne *Sea Birds (Gulls in Newlyn Harbour)*
87 Knight Harold *The Council* study
54 Millard Fred *Cornish Girl with Primroses*
57 Rheam Henry Meynell *Gathering Daffodils*
56 Suthers Leghe *Anne Rowney of Newlyn*
32 Todd Ralph *Harvesters of the Sea*
96 Walke Anne *Christ Mocked*
97 Walke Anne *Rev Bernard Walke and his Mother*

Photographic Credits

All photographic credits rest with the galleries or collections listed in the captions except Frank Bramley A *Hopeless Dawn*© Tate, London 2002

Copyright Credits